T5-CQA-926

Designer Genes
Ken Abraham

BY Ken Abraham
Don't Bite the Apple 'Til You Check for Worms
Designer Genes

Designer Genes
Ken Abraham

Power
Books

Fleming H. Revell Company
Old Tappan, New Jersey

Unless otherwise identified, Scripture quotations in this volume are from the New American Standard Bible, © The Lockman Foundation, 1960, 1962, 1963, 1968, 1971, 1972, 1973, 1975, 1977.

Verses marked TLB are taken from *The Living Bible*, Copyright © 1971 by Tyndale House Publishers, Wheaton, Ill. Used by permission.

Scripture quotations identified NIV are from Holy Bible, New International Version, copyright © 1978, New York International Bible Society. Used by permission.

Library of Congress Cataloging-in-Publication Data

Abraham, Ken.
  Designer genes.

  1. Christian life—1960–   . I. Title.
BV4501.2.A2   1986   248.4   86-11833
ISBN 0-8007-5224-4

Copyright © 1986 by Ken Abraham
Published by Fleming H. Revell Company
Old Tappan, New Jersey 07675
All Rights Reserved
Printed in the United States of America

TO
My mom and dad,
Minnie and Howard Abraham,
from whom I inherited far more
than physical genes. They passed on to me
their zest for living and their loving adoration
of the Designer.

Thanks, Mom and Dad.
I love you!

Contents

Contents

Prologue

There's a craze in fashion
That's taking the world by storm
Even though the price is hard to pay.
Now, if you're gonna make it
With the social set in town,
You better have a label
On everything you wear!

Now I'm not knockin' fashion,
Or your trying to dress in style,
Even though that might be what it seems.
No, I'm just trying to tell you
That before you were even born,
God Himself gave you Designer Genes!

(*Chorus*)
Well, you've got Designer Genes!
You're really one of a kind!
Designer Genes, conceived in God's own mind;
One of God's unique creations.
Don't accept cheap imitations!
You've got the best Designer Genes!

9

Prologue

You've got Jordache on your pocket,
Calvin Klein on your sleeve;
Can't you see it's all an illusion,
Just a world of make-believe?
Well, you can't find Zechariah,
But you never miss Saint Laurent.
You know, there's nothing wrong with being in style,
But can't you see the mess you're in?
Well, you think Jovan is a heavenly scent,
Ya buy Oscar de la Renta cologne;
Now, if this song steps on your toes,
Ooh! I beg your Chardon!

Well, you might be old and faded,
In need of a patch or two,
You might feel like you're tearin' at the seams.
Then give your life to Jesus;
Let Him wash you through and through.
He'll give you back some fresh Designer Genes!

Repeat Chorus

Words by Ken Abraham, Music by Tink Abraham. Copyright © 1982 Evergreen Music Group, Clymer, PA 15728. International Copyright Secured. All Rights Reserved. Used by Permission.

Designer Genes
Ken Abraham

The Designer Generation

The first time I tried on a pair of designer jeans, I was the easiest sale in the store. . . .

"Nice choice! Those jeans will look super on you!" the vibrant, young saleswoman commented, as she noticed my selection. She appeared to be about twenty-two years old, with sparkling blue eyes and long, golden-blond hair that curled innocently, yet somehow seductively, around her shoulders. She was stylishly dressed, and I instantly recognized her as a woman of taste.

"You can try them on right in here," she pointed to a cubbyhole adjacent to the clothing racks.

"Er, ah . . . well, I was just looking, actually . . . do you really think they'd look that good? I mean . . . oh, well; okay. I may as well."

The magnetic saleswoman smiled and unlocked the door. "Take your time," she said, holding the door for me.

I ducked into the department-store dressing room, wondering as I went, *Why do they always have the pretty girls working in the Men's Department?* I pulled the dark blue pants onto my frame, zipped them up, and quickly exited the cramped compartment. I was anxious to see what the expensive fabric did for me.

Outside the dressing room stood a semicircle of mirrors. I stepped into the focal point, where I could see myself from as many different angles as possible.

Hmm, not bad! I thought, as I gazed admiringly at the multiple images of the person in the mirrors. *These jeans really do fit well, I have to admit.* I had heard that "the fit" was one of the main reasons why the designer-jeans craze was catching on so rapidly. At least, that was the excuse everyone used for shelling out so much money for these high-priced, fancy pants.

"Wow! You look terrific!" my saleswoman's enthusiastic, titillating voice interrupted my thoughts.

"Do you really think so?" I asked sheepishly.

"Are you kidding?" She continued. "You look like a new man!" She came closer and walked all around me, rubbing her fingers on her chin, as if she was contemplating the purchase of a new car. I could smell the fresh scent of her blond hair as she circled me.

She paused, stepped back about three feet, and gave me a once-over glance from head to toe. "You know, you're lucky."

"I am?"

"You certainly are. Not everyone can wear these new designer styles."

"They can't?"

"No, you see, designer jeans fit so well, if you don't have a good body underneath, you might look pretty silly. I mean, on some people, the jeans you are wearing might accentuate their poor shape. You know what I mean?"

"Huh? Ahhh, yeah, well; I mean, I guess so." I could feel my face beginning to get warm. I was grateful when she continued her sales pitch.

14

"But on you," she paused again, taking time for another head-to-toe examination, "those jeans just make you look all the more sleek and slender."

I stood up straighter and stretched my chest so she wouldn't notice my pudgies hidden ever so discreetly beneath the waistband of my new-found wonder pants. "Sleek and slender, huh?"

"Mmm-hmm," she oozed, her voice barely above a whisper. "Sleek and slender."

"Ah-hem; yes . . ." I responded nervously stepping away from the woman and back toward the mirrors. My face was hot crimson, and I could feel a trickle of sweat sneaking down the small of my back. I looked into the glass again and thought, *You know, these jeans* do *make me look sleek and slender!*

"Er, ah . . . how much are they?" I ventured.

My saleswoman was suddenly all business as she swished around in front of me. "Well, normally," she answered, "they sell for ninety dollars."

"Ninety bucks!" I almost choked.

"Ah-hem, yes; ninety dollars." I thought I detected a touch of condescension in her tone and in her look. "But," she continued, her smile brightening as she spoke, "this must be your lucky day!"

"Oh?"

"Yes; today is our half-price sale! All of our new designer jeans are on sale for one day only!"

"Half-price?" I queried. "Forty-five bucks?"

"Yes," she replied, her enthusiasm back in full force. "Today, you can have these beautiful designer jeans for only forty-five dollars. You're worth forty-five dollars, aren't you?" Her white teeth flashed again as she spoke. We both knew she had me at this point, but I wasn't giving in so easily. I looked back to the mirrors once more.

"Well, they do make me look sleek and slender, and they are on sale; so they cost forty-five bucks? So what? I'm worth it. . . ." I was sounding more like a television commercial every second, so I resigned myself to the inevitable. "Do you take Master Card or American Express?" I managed to squeak out.

"Both," the woman answered majestically.

"It figures," I replied. I reentered the claustrophobic cubicle and quickly began changing back into my worn but comfortable $12.95 Plain Pockets.

I paid the saleswoman for my designer jeans and jubilantly glided out the door. *Well, that's a pretty good bargain,* I rationalized, as I hopped into my car and placed my newest status symbol on the seat next to me. *"Instant status." And all for only forty-five bucks!*

Material Whirl

Today, young adults are more status conscious concerning the way they look and dress than any generation in history. They consume colossal amounts of time, energy, and money, feverishly striving to improve the appearance of their hair, their complexions, and their physiques. Why? Because peer pressure and media pressure tell us that we must look younger, more beautiful, more stylish than ever if we intend to make it in the Big World out there. Consequently, young people are lining up at Nautilus equipment, beauty shops, and tanning salons in record numbers.

Once the physical body is pounded or pampered into semi-acceptable shape, then it becomes imperative that you package the New Look in proper fashion. After all, this is the "Designer Generation." It's not *what* you are wearing that counts; the primary concern among style-conscious youth these days is *who* you are wearing. You've got to sport the right label if you expect to fit in with the movers and shakers.

Glance around any high school cafeteria or college dining room and what do you see? Labels. Labels! Designer labels! They're everywhere! No Salvation Army cast-offs here. The Designer Generation has class—and expensive tastes.

Doug is wearing his faded Levi 501 dungarees. They haven't faded from repeated washings; Doug paid extra money for that washed-out look.

Shelly has on her new black stirrup pants, just like the kind Amy Grant wears.

Guess jeans and Reebok or Ellesse sneakers, topped with posh Fila shirts adorn upper classmen.

Sophomore girls all have (somewhere in their wardrobes!) at least one sweat shirt with the word *Esprit* emblazoned on it. Hardly anyone knows what *Esprit* means, but that's okay. It's in style.

Expensive, colorful, T-shirts announce everything from one's sexual/social status (I'M A VIRGIN) to favorite rock groups (DURAN DURAN, PETRA, or STRYPER), to preferred modes of transportation (HARLEY, SUZUKI, or HONDA). Jocks, or aspiring jocks, proudly display their Adidas, Nike, or Etonic tennis shoes. In days past, advertisers would have paid plenty for such flagrant commercial proliferation. Now, we gladly pay them for the privilege of wearing their logos!

How did this designer craze get started? Some say Brooke Shields set the fires blazing by posing half-naked in nothing but her Calvin Klein jeans. Others point to afternoon television soap operas and prime-time soaps such as "Dynasty" and "Dallas" as leading sources of stylish stimulation. Rock musicians and MTV now set the trends for younger teens.

However it began, the American consumer's voracious appetite to gobble up anything bearing a designer's label did not go unnoticed by Madison Avenue. Soon stores were overloaded with "one of a kind" products by Bill Blass, Yves Saint Laurent, Evan-Picone, Oscar de la Renta, Ralph Lauren, Liz Claiborne, Gloria Vanderbilt, Jordache, Pierre Cardin, and a host of other names, many of which were unfamiliar to us. Never fear! We were assured by zealous salesclerks that these newcomers were, indeed, prestigious labels. "Everybody who is anybody is wearing it," the message was incessantly driven into our brains.

Meanwhile, mail-order catalogs also joined the designer deluge. Catalogs from Bloomingdales, Neiman-Marcus, and Saks Fifth Avenue peppered the mail, helping to keep post-teens aware of tomorrow's fads and fashions in the rapid-paced designer's world. Now even staid penny pinchers such as Sears, J. C. Penney's, and Spiegel, once havens for the workaday, price-conscious shopper, have gone Hollywood on us, grappling to grab the Designer Generation's greenbacks.

The designers, whoever they may be, have duped us into desiring a designer's image—*their* image—of what the Designer Generation should be. To be accepted nowadays, we gladly pay anywhere from twenty-five to eighty-five dollars for a pair of jeans, flaunting some ostensibly famous person's name on the pocket. We reek of designer fragrances. We write with designer ink pens. We carry our designer suits, belts, ties, and underwear in our designer luggage. We drive designer edition automobiles. Wearing our designer shoes and jackets, we walk our papered and pedigreed pups, reining the pooch in on his or her designer dog collar!

If you or I could only invent a Designer Burger, or Designer Antifreeze, I know we'd never have to work another day in our lives!

Funny thing about the Designer Generation: this is the same crowd that says, "Hey! I gotta be me!" We hear it all the time, don't we?

"I don't want to be like anybody else"
"I'm not just a cog in a machine."
"I've gotta be myself. Different. Unique!"
"I'm an individualist."

Amazing, isn't it? In an age where we are crying out against conformity and sameness, idolizing our individuality, the so-called in crowd is still trying to establish its identity by wearing somebody else's label! Maybe the strangest thing is that we are all starting to look somewhat the same, more or less monotonous, almost like a community of clones.

The Designer Generation wears the same haircut, the same suntan, and, of course, the same designer clothes. For all our talk about self-expression and personal freedom, we have become boringly banal. We are most comfortable and secure when we are in familiar territory, easily labeled and identified, and easily recognized. The Designer Generation talks a lot about "doing your own thing" and future successes, but because of their fear of failure and the constant pressure to look perfect, they have become a bland and blasé group, unaccustomed to experimentation or risk taking.

Many modern-day youth won't even raise their hands in class to answer a question—not because they don't know the answer, but their self-images have been so battered, they are reluctant to venture even that far out on their own. In most classrooms, the students sit in a group, looking like they are plaster of paris statues that have been placed onto the chairs. The teacher can preach radical, profound, and sometimes controversial concepts to them, and the Designer Generation won't even blink. They're laid back, uncommitted. If Joe the Jock, sitting in the corner with his feet propped up on the chair in front of him, finds something funny and lets out a laugh, the other kids might laugh too—but not until. If Glenda the Glamorous groans, several other students will groan with her—but not until.

It's not that the Designer Generation is ignorant or disinterested. On the contrary, these are some of the brightest, sharpest young people ever! It's just that for many of them, their self-esteem has been so beaten into the ground, they won't even attempt to express themselves in a group of more than two or three other friends.

Their credo is, "Let somebody else stick his [or her] neck out—not me!" Their philosophy is sort of like the old Cowboys and Indians Method of Research: if you send a scout out and he comes back shot full of arrows, you say, "Well, I guess that's not a good place to be!"

Consequently, the Designer Generation has become paralyzed by indecision. Nobody wants to take responsibility if things don't pan out just right. Everyone would rather sit back and wait for someone else to tell them what to do. Follow the Leader has become much more than a childhood game. It is now a way of life. The leader may be the local sports hero, or the local pothead, or the latest pop music star, and it is to this demagogue the Designer Generation has abdicated decision making, thrusting it into the oftentimes incompetent hands of the high-profile personality. Role models (although rather strange ones) are back in style.

"Hey, man, if Bruce Springsteen said it, I believe it."

"Rambo for President!"

"The new Miss America is . . . Cyndi Lauper."

Unique or You're Not

Sometimes, fitting in gets to be a bit bewildering. You have to really know what's in and what's out, what's hot and what's not.

At first, Amber began to sob quietly, when Dr. Stennis told her that she would have to have braces placed on her teeth. However, as Dr. Stennis continued instructing her about the brackets and elastic bands she would be wearing, Amber's sobs turned into a stream of tears.

"Now, now," Dr. Stennis attempted to console her. "Lots of kids your age have to wear braces for a while. It's only a temporary condition. When it's over, you'll have wonderfully straight teeth. There's no need to be upset."

The dentist's words only caused Amber's tears to continue. Undaunted, Dr. Stennis tried a different tack. "I know that in days past, some nasty nicknames were given to people who wore braces. Names like 'Tinmouth,' and 'Tinsel teeth,' and 'Jaws,' but Amber, it's certainly nothing to cry about!"

"Oh, Doctor," Amber answered through her sobbing. "You don't understand! I'm not crying because I'm sad. I'm crying because I'm *glad!* Now, I can finally look like all the other kids in my class!"

Brad, a high school senior, summed up the spirit of the times: "No matter what, you've got to look like you belong, like you know what's happenin'. To be avoided at all costs is looking or acting like someone who just came in from outta town!"

Some individualism, huh? That's not being unique or different; that's *conformity.* And it's conformity of the most demeaning sort, simply acquiescing to the crass, clamoring of the crowd.

That's one of the reasons why I'm a Christian. Christians are different. Not weird—different. If you're weird, that's your own fault; don't blame God for that. I'm talking about being set apart from the maddening masses.

Perhaps the most liberating part of the Good News is that we don't have to be *just like everyone else* in order to "make it." As a Christian, you can be free from all that! You don't have to derive your sense of self-worth from society's status symbols. God thought you were important enough and of such immense value, that He gave His only Son, Jesus, to Calvary's cross, so you might be free. *Really* free.

Furthermore, long before the earth was formed (over four billion years ago, some scientists say), God had in mind a marvelous design for your life. Before you were even born, God put His stamp of approval upon you; He put *His* label on you so you could be forever free from all others.

King David, a most insightful poet and songwriter, put it this way in a song of praise and thanks directed toward his Designer:

21

You made all the delicate, inner parts of my body,
and knit them together in my mother's womb.
Thank you for making me so wonderfully complex!
It is amazing to think about. Your workmanship is
marvelous—and how well I know it. You were there
while I was being formed in utter seclusion! You saw
me before I was born and scheduled each day of my
life before I began to breathe. Every day was recorded in your Book!

Psalms 139:13–16 TLB

Think about that! The Grandest Designer of all created an
original masterpiece—*you!* You are not a copy of anyone else.
You are a unique individual. You are not a forgery, or a
pseudounique creation, as are many of the so-called designer
fashions.

The Master Designer didn't simply make one mold, and
then mass-produce all other humans that have ever lived.

No. You are a one-of-a-kind classic! An original. An unre-
peatable miracle. You have your own style, your own smile,
your own unique fingerprints, and your own voice prints. From
the moment of your conception, the genes and chromosomes
that make up your body have been so arranged by your heavenly Father that no other person on earth is quite like you.
God Himself created you and endowed you with *Designer
Genes.*

Angela, my wife, and I love to visit art galleries. Once, we
spent an entire day, simply browsing through the National Art
Gallery in Washington, D.C. As we strolled through the cav-
ernous corridors, I noted that there were security guards posted
in almost every room. I couldn't help wondering, *What makes
these paintings so valuable that they would merit such scrupu-
lous attention and protection?* Was it merely because they
were done by such artists as Renoir, Picasso, Rembrandt,

Cézanne, Van Gogh, Matisse, and others? What grants them their esteemed status in those hallowed halls?

Then it hit me. Each painting that I was so casually perusing was an original creation, done by a skilled master artist. These were not cheap numbered prints. These were not mass reproductions. Each rare piece of art had inestimable value for two reasons; one, because it was unique and could never be replaced; and second, because of the immeasurable greatness of the artist who had created each work.

You and I are much like those paintings. We have been handcrafted by God as a rare treasure. The Bible says, "We are His workmanship, created in Christ Jesus for good works, which God prepared beforehand, that we should walk in them" (Ephesians 2:10).

There has never been and will never be another of God's masterpieces just like you! That fact alone should give you an enormous sense of value for yourself and gratitude toward God.

If you are an original masterpiece, and there will never be another you, why should you want to be like someone else? You don't have to be! The Master Designer has given *you* unique gifts, talents, and personality traits to be used for His glory. God doesn't want you to be a cheap reproduction of someone else. He made you, and He loves you! He wants you to be the very best *you* that you can possibly be.

Life-styles of the Rich and Famous

Aren't you glad that you don't have to gauge your sense of self-worth and value according to the standards of the world! People who attempt to attain success in the eyes of secular society find themselves on a never-ending treadmill.

After all, how many of us are going to be "somebodies" in society's system? In the world's hierarchy, how many of us are ever going to escape obscurity and "make it big"? I don't want to burst your bubble or give you an excuse for mediocrity, but the truthful answer is: "Only a few."

How many star quarterbacks can there be at one school? How many head cheerleaders, featured baton twirlers, or valedictorians can one school stand? The Beautiful Bodies and the Intellectual Giants and the Super Achievers make up a miniscule portion of the total USA population. As such, if you buy into the Designer Generation's standards of success, you better realize that the system itself is geared toward creating "nobodies" rather than "somebodies."

How does the Designer Generation describe success? In dollars and cents? In power? In fame? Well, yes, but there are a few other ways, as well. Besides being known worldwide by your first name or nickname (Farrah, Elvis, Pele, Raquel, Barbra, the Duke, or Prince, to name a few), Russell Reid has noted five familiar fame factors in an article in *Republic* magazine, "How to Tell if You're Really Famous."

1. "You know you've made it when you are a guest on the 'Tonight Show.'" (Of course, Johnny only features approximately 1,250 guest appearances each year, so your chances of making it there are about one in 184,000 Americans!)

2. "Another assurance of success is when you see your name in *Who's Who in America.*" (True, you have to rack up some pretty impressive accomplishments in order to be listed among the elite seventy-five thousand entries in the annual volume. Still your odds are better here than most places—one person for every three thousand Americans gets listed in this prestigious book.)

3. "One of the most coveted honors for any celebrity on the make," reports Reid, "would be a star appearance on the cover of *People* magazine."

(Can't you just picture yourself right now? There you are, smiling out at the millions of supermarket shoppers as they push and shove through the checkout counters of America. Pretty heady stuff! Unfortunately, *People* only creates 50 covers per year, so your chances of gracing it approach one shot in 4.5 million!)

4. "Of course, you could leave your footprints in the cement at Mann's [formerly Grauman's] Chinese Theater in Hollywood." (But by the time they run out of sidewalk squares, only one person in 1.15 million will have attained that status.)

5. Oh, yes. There is one other way to tell that you've really made it, according to Reid. When the *New York Times* features you in a front-page obituary story, you will have achieved the dubious distinction that only one in 7.6 million Americans can share. (Of course, by the time the *Times* prints your story, you won't be around to read it!)

Whew! Aren't you glad that as Christians we can be free from the Designer Generation's superficial attitudes toward success! We don't have to seek after status symbols to prove that we are somebodies. Our Master Designer has already declared us to be *somebodies.* And God doesn't lie, so we know it's true.

What we want to discover through *Designer Genes* is how to live in alignment with what He says about you, not by what the system says, your classmates say, or even what your best friends and relatives say about you. Nobodies try to achieve success and happiness through their wallets, their looks, brains, position, or prestige. Somebodies know that we don't have to *earn* our self-worth; God has already freely given to us the greatest gift of all, apart from Jesus. He has bestowed upon us a self worth loving, a self worth respecting, a self worth improving, a self worth utilizing for our greatest enjoyment and for His greatest glory. The Grand Designer says, "Hey! I kind of like you. In fact, I love you! You have intrinsic, infinite value to Me."

Here is the bad news and the good news of the Gospel. The bad news is that the Designer Generation, languishing in saturation level luxury, lust, and riches, is a bankrupt system (*See* Revelation 3:17). It's empty. Void. The members of the Designer Generation are frustrated and confused; they can't seem to find their own identity, no matter how many success labels they acquire.

On the other hand, the good news is that the Designer Genes Generation is beginning to take hold. Many modern Christian young adults are discovering the truth, that God labels us differently than the world does, that the only niche you need to fit into is the one your Designer made especially for you. In fact, our Omnipotent Creator despises our attempts to squeeze all of His diverse, original creations into the same glass of orange juice. That's why the apostle Paul wrote, "Do not be conformed to this world, but be transformed by the renewing of your mind, that you may prove what the will of God is, that which is good and acceptable and perfect" (Romans 12:2).

Here, we see two vital principles that govern the realization of our full potential as Designer Genes people:

1. Don't be conformed to this world! You are unique, so dare to be different; dare to be *yourself!*

2. Be transformed by the renewing of your mind. Let's allow God to renew our mental attitudes and self-images according to His Word.

You don't need Calvin, Gloria, or Oscar to make it as a Designer Genes person. You just need Jesus.

So come alive! Join the Designer Genes Generation. Keep reading and let me show you how to realize your fullest potential as a Designer Genes person.

Inside Out

Now you have some information on the inside, but head knowledge alone will not significantly alter your life-style. It has to be incorporated into your day-to-day living. That's what "Inside Out" is all about.

At the end of each chapter, you will find questions you can use for self-analysis, thought stimulation, and group discussion. Some of the questions will challenge you to do something now—*today!* Others will challenge you to trust your Designer for greater achievements than you have ever dreamed possible. Don't be bashful about living up to His greatest potential for you.

Inside Out for
"The Designer Generation"

1. *List your favorite designers. When you purchase a product, what determines your selection? The brand name? Quality? Price? Style? Usefulness? Other?*

2. *Describe the silliest designer product you have ever seen.*

3. *What impresses you most when you meet a person for the first time? Personal appearance? Personality? Be specific.*

4. *Who is more important to God, the person who wears expensive clothes and drives a fancy car, or the person that wears hand-me-downs and rides the bus?*

5. *Describe a time when you felt inferior because you couldn't buy your clothes at the "right" store. How does your experience relate to Matthew 6:25–34?*

6. *Have you ever bought an imitation designer product because you couldn't afford the real thing? How did you feel about doing that? What impression were you trying to make?*

7. *If you won a five-thousand-dollar shopping spree at an exclusive department store, what would you buy?*

8. *How much value will your wardrobe have ten years from now? One hundred years from today? One million years from now?*

9. *Read Genesis 1:26, 27. In your own words, describe what these verses mean to you.*

10. *Name three qualities, uniquely yours, that make you different from anyone else.*

11. *As you go through your day, notice other people and observe how delightfully unique your Designer has created each of us to be. Give Him thanks and praise for His originality.*

12. *Your Designer has placed some labels on you. Relate each of the labels to the Scriptures given:*
      • Exclusive, *An original creation (Genesis 2:1–3)*
      • Made in God's Image *(Genesis 1:26)*
      • Washing Instructions *(Acts 22:16; Titus 3:5; Isaiah 1:16)*
      • Custom-made, *(Romans 8:29, Ephesians 2:10).*

What are some other labels your Designer has placed upon you?

Potentially Yours

I am often invited to speak at baccalaureate and graduation ceremonies, and as far as possible, I always accept. I consider it to be part of my continuing education.

Each spring, I watch thousands of high school and college graduates collect their diplomas, have a wild party with friends (or a more sedate dinner with Mom and Dad), and then sink into the abyss of the Real World, never to be heard from again. And I wonder *Why?*

Some of these graduates have studied diligently and have crammed their brains full of facts for twelve, sixteeen, nineteen years, or more—only to become highly educated waitresses, stockboys, and door-to-door salesmen. Some will become computer programmers; some will become accountants; others will become math teachers, electrical engineers, pastors, stock brokers, or social workers. A lot won't do anything at all with their lives. And I wonder, *Why not?*

What happened during those crucial years of maturation and preparation? Why are some graduates ready and willing to go out and meet the world head-on, while others prefer to hide out in the locker room for the rest of their lives? They all have such tremendous potential! What makes the difference between the winners and losers—those who live up to their potential—and those who don't?

Three elements constitute that curious compound known as your potential: *Talent, knowledge,* and *desire.* All three are important, but it is no secret that individuals can often make up for a lack of natural-born talent by increasing their knowledge or by intensifying their desire. When the three ingredients are poured into the same person, you have enormous potential.

Dwight Gooden is a good example. The winsome twenty-one-year-old baseball pitcher for the New York Mets was named the National League's "Rookie of the Year" in 1984. In 1985, Dwight topped that by winning the coveted Cy Young Award, the honor that goes to baseball's best hurler, after he led the major leagues in strikeouts (268) and won 24 games for the Mets.

In his gracious manner, Gooden explained his success. "Basically," he says, "I think it's just God-gifted talent. Plus, when you get in tough situations, like the bases loaded and nobody out, you never give in. Just keep feeling like you're the best out there. You got the ball in your hands and you're in command . . ." (*People,* December 23, 1985, p. 77).

Talent Search

Talents are God-given gifts or abilities. You didn't have a lot to do with the original list of gifts you were given by your Designer. God miraculously combined twenty-three chromosomes from your mother and twenty-three chromosomes from your father, and *you* were the composite result! You had no choice over which genes you inherited, those that would influence your general shape, size, bone structure, skin color, and intelligence. You were simply born with or without certain characteristics. You are, however, responsible to God, and to society and to yourself for what you have done with the talents, gifts, and abilities that were given to you.

We all have different talents, and sometimes it takes a little time and experimentation to find that at which we are best. Don't get discouraged if your first few attempts don't set your heart fluttering.

When I was six years old, my mother enrolled me in violin classes. I never had an overdose of natural talent for playing the thing, but I was enthralled with the idea of playing a musical instrument. I dreamed of someday being a professional musician, so I poured myself into practice.

Every afternoon at 4:00 I would get out my bow and start grating it across the strings. Windows throughout our neighborhood suddenly slammed shut; dogs who were previously the pride of their owners, the epitome of discipline, breeding, and training, began yelping uncontrollably. Radio signals jammed. Television screens turned to snow. Many assumed that the horrible screeching sounds were the precursors to a Russian nuclear attack. The Emergency Broadcasting Network flew into action! Meanwhile, I contentedly continued drawing the horsehair bow over the metal strings, thinking all the time that I was making great music.

The entire world (it seemed) breathed a sigh of relief when one day I looked at my violin in despair and said, "This squawk box is going to take too much work to learn how to play! I quit."

Believe me, the earth is now a better place to live.

Next I tried trumpet lessons. I was a natural spitter, so I felt confident that I could develop the tongue action required to play like Doc Severinsen. Each evening, my dad took me up to the bathroom to practice. I could never figure out why we practiced amid all the porcelain facilities, but for some reason, my father decided that that room was the most appropriate environment for my trumpet playing.

Not surprisingly, by the time I finished fourth grade, I'd had enough potty training! My trumpet days were over.

After that, I immersed myself in baseball and football, temporarily forgetting all about my dream to be a professional musician. One day, nearly five years later, I picked up a set of drum sticks and found that I was much better at banging drum heads, than I was at banging helmet heads. I was on my way. I had found my niche.

Talent is an important factor in potential, but untapped talent is useless. Have you ever seen a gifted individual who you knew was not living up to his or her potential? Why not?

Maybe this person was just plain lazy. Laziness looms as one of the largest stumbling blocks for naturally gifted individuals. The more talent a person has, the greater the temptation to be lazy. Why? Because things come more easily to them than to the person who has less natural ability.

I gave Jeff a ride home from school one day during midterms. I knew he was a straight A student, so I was surprised that he was going home empty-handed.

"Jeff," I asked, "don't you have any tests to study for?"

"Yeah, I've got three tomorrow," he answered calmly.

"But you don't have any books! Aren't you going to study?" I pressed.

"Oh, sure, I guess so. But I've got a study hall in the morning. That should be all the time I need. These courses are a piece of cake anyhow."

I knew the young man was right. He could probably do better without studying than most of his classmates would do after pulling an all-nighter. Still, I couldn't help prodding, "Jeff, if you ever applied yourself, just think how far you might go! You could graduate early, or maybe explore other areas where your interests lie. You could sit in on some college courses, or take some specialized studies, geared to your intelligence level."

His answer was disappointing. "No," he said. "I just do enough to get along. Just what is necessary and not inconvenient."

The cult of the comfortable worships at the golden calf of convenience and complacency. However, young people who know they have been given Designer Genes want to go further.

They want to be good stewards of God's great gifts to them, whether success comes easily, with a minimum of exertion, or when it is something we have to sweat and sacrifice to reach.

I admire performers and songwriters Michael Jackson and Paul McCartney, not simply because they are among our world's premier music talents, but because they continue to refine, develop, and exercise their gifts long after they have reached the pinnacle of success in their field. How easy it would be for Michael or Paul to simply take their millions of dollars and live quietly and comfortably anywhere in the world. But they haven't done so. They continue to write, to record, to create, constantly working to be better at their craft. Sure, they risk rejection every time they put out a new piece of music, but that risk is far less than what burying their talents in the sand would be.

Use It or Lose It

Do you remember the Parable of the Talents in Matthew 25:14–30? The master gave one fellow ten talents, another five, and another he gave one talent. A talent was worth about a thousand dollars.

The first two invested their talents and when the master returned, they were given an appropriate reward. The fellow who had the least to lose was too timid to do anything with what had been entrusted to him. He simply buried the talent, and when the master came back, dug it out and gave it back to him. This man, however, received a scathing rebuke, rather than a reward.

Though the talents in this story were measures of money, the principle governs the stewardship of every gift, ability, and resource our God has given to us. It's the old "use it or lose it" adage. Either use what the Lord has given to you for His glory, or it will be taken away from you and given to someone else.

If you are naturally talented, great! Give thanks and praise to your Designer for granting those special genes to you. You are going to be a great artist, because you are gifted. You're going to be a star running back, because God gave you strong legs and good speed.

Whether you are extraordinarily gifted or not, however, always keep in mind: it's not aptitude that counts the most—it's your attitude. Always make the best of what God has given you. He will be pleased with you, and you will be pleased with yourself.

When I speak in high schools, I often ask students, "How many of you can run a marathon?"

Most of the young people automatically respond with: "No way! I'd drop after the first quarter mile!"

"Marathon? Are you kidding? If I have to run to the bus, I'm in big trouble!"

Yet, if most of those same students *wanted* to run in a marathon, they could, assuming they were willing to train, practice, and prepare. Attitude makes the difference.

When Arnold Schwarzenegger, the famous body builder, wanted to become an actor, he was turned down on three counts. First, he was told his body was too big and muscular to be a movie star. (How would you like to have been the fellow who had to tell Arnold *that?*) Second, he had a foreign accent and often spoke in broken or poor English. Third, his advisors suggested that he change his name.

"This is America, Arnold. Schwarzenegger just doesn't make it. Redford, Reynolds, or Hoffman, maybe, but Schwarzenegger . . . never!"

Arnold was undaunted. He set about the task of trimming his body down, so it wouldn't look excessively muscular. (What a nice problem!) He did so by adjusting his eating and exercising habits. At the same time, he began to study the English language and struggled to improve his enunciation. Arnold stood his ground, however, when it came to changing his name. Instead, he vowed to make Schwarzenegger a household name.

Today, Arnold Schwarzenegger is as popular for his movies as he was for body building. He's no ninety-pound weakling, and his movies don't exactly tax his vocabulary, but he's doing what he wants to do with his life. His name? Well, it's still not a household name, but Maria Shriver, whose family name (Kennedy) *is* familiar to most Americans, doesn't mind. She consented to marry Arnold. It's all in your attitude, isn't it?

What Can One Person Do?

Have you ever heard yourself or one of your friends say, "Hey! What can *I* do? I'm only one person. What kind of impact can *I* have? I can't make a difference, so I won't do anything." This perennial problem of youth is called *apathy*. It's been with us since the beginning of time. No doubt, Adam and Eve probably said, "These kids nowadays are so apathetic; they don't care about anything!"

Jay Kessler, president of Taylor University in Indiana and former president of Youth for Christ, points out that there is a major difference in attitude among modern young people compared to past generations. Says Kessler, "Today's teenagers are apathetic, not because they don't know enough to care about the world; they're apathetic because they know just enough about the world to think that they don't matter" (from "The Return of Apathy," an interview with Jay Kessler by Gregg Lewis, in *Christianity Today*, October 18, 1985). It's not so much an "I don't care" attitude, Kessler explains further, as it is a "What can *I* do about it" feeling.

"What can *I* do about nuclear war?"
"What can *I* do about acid rain?"
"What can *I* do about a faltering economy?"
"What can *I* do about a million abortions a year?"
"What can *I* do about thousands of human beings starving to death right this moment?"

It's easy to fall into that sort of apathetic trap, isn't it? Yet, as Tony Campolo says, "You *can* make a difference!" One person *can* have a tremendous impact!

Have you ever heard of Bob Geldof? Possibly not. He was just another foul-mouthed rock star, until a short time ago when he saw a need and felt impressed that he had to do something about it. He could not ignore the plight of starving children in Africa any longer. But what could a musician do about malnutrition and starvation? Geldof decided to do what he did best; he'd make music! To help him, he sought out the most popular musicians in Europe and, together, they launched what is now known as "Band Aid" with their first effort, "Do They Know It's Christmas?" Doing what "little" they could, the musicians raised over ten million dollars to help relieve hunger in Africa.

In the United States, Harry Belafonte caught wind of Band Aid's European success. Who could ever have thought that it would be possible to organize a video project involving Stevie Wonder, Bob Dylan, Kenny Rogers, Cyndi Lauper, Willie Nelson, Diana Ross, Bruce Springsteen, Lionel Richie, Paul Simon, Michael Jackson, and a cavalcade of other music superstars? Who would ever have dreamed that you could get all these stars on one record? Better yet, one song? Who would believe? Well, Bob Geldof did, for one. And Harry Belafonte, for two.

Who would believe that it would be possible to arrange for each talent to be donated free of charge? Bob and Harry did! Who would ever imagine that radio stations all over the world would play "We Are the World" simultaneously? Bob and Harry did! Who could possibly imagine that fifty of pop music's biggest performers, including personalities as diverse as Paul McCartney, Mick Jagger, and U2, would band together for two concerts, dubbed as "Live Aid," and broadcast to more than a billion people worldwide over radio and TV? Who else? And what were these superstars paid? Not a penny. In fact, U2 estimated that it cost *them* over $15,000 to participate in the project ("Music News," *Rolling Stone*, David Fricke, August 15, 1985).

Yet, because Bob Geldof believed that one person *can* make a difference, Live Aid has raised over 92 million dollars. Following the lead of Geldof and Belafonte, other individuals have jumped on the "Band-wagon." As a result, literally millions of dollars have been raised to help relieve famine-racked Ethiopia and other parts of Africa.

Can one person have an impact? Ask Bob Geldof.

Use the talent your Designer has given you. Nobody else can do what you can do. Maybe you can't help millions of starving people, but you may be able to save the life of one person. In my church, I often recommend that young people pool their resources to help support a needy child through World Vision, Compassion International, or some similar Christian relief oganization. What a thrill it is to see these young people get involved in helping to alleviate the plight of another person.

Maybe you can't visit everyone who is sick or alone in a hospital or nursing home, but I'll bet there is an old, lonely woman or man somewhere in your town who is looking out the window right now, longing for someone to come and share a little love with them. You can be that someone.

You may not be able to change the whole world, but if you use your talent for God's glory, you might just change *your* world!

What Do You Know?

The second main component of your potential is *knowledge*. This includes your current skills, education, and training.

Many people do not live life to their fullest potential because they fail to realize what a fantastic gift our Designer has given to us in the human brain. It is often said that our minds are the fastest working, coolest running, most compact and efficient computer mechanisms ever created!

The Brain Research Institute at UCLA would certainly

agree. According to their studies, the creative learning capacity of your brain may be *infinite*. That's right—*infinite!* Recent research has discovered that we have more than 100 billion neuron cells in our brains; each *one* of these neuron cells can store more data than the most sophisticated computer on earth. You may not believe that when you can't find your car keys, or you can't remember who fought whom in the Battle of Waterloo, but it's true.

A popular program on television currently is a show called "Riptide." In it, two good-looking hunks are assisted in their private detective agency by a twirpy-looking (but genius) computer wiz, named Boz.

Undoubtedly, the expert writer of "Riptide" scripts, Stephen Cannell, has hit upon a key insight for our futures. Nowadays, and in the years ahead, it won't be enough to be cool, good-looking, or strong; you're going to need some brains to go along with the brawn. Knowledge is—and will be—*power*.

As Christians, we should understand that "The fear of the LORD is the beginning of knowledge . . ." (Proverbs 1:7). A reverential awe of the Designer who created the incredible computer between your ears will cause you to want to make good use of His gift to you. Can you believe it? God wants you to study and obtain knowledge and wisdom.

The Bible is replete with encouragement to seek godly wisdom. For example:

> Get wisdom, get understanding; do not forget my words or swerve from them. Do not forsake wisdom, and she will protect you; love her, and she will watch over you. Wisdom is supreme; therefore get wisdom. Though it cost all you have, get understanding. Esteem her, and she will exalt you; embrace her, and she will honor you. She will set a garland of grace on your head and present you with a crown of splendor.
>
> Proverbs 4:5–9 NIV

Knowledge and wisdom, however, like talent, are useless unless you put them to work for you. Here is a simple test to see how well you are using what you know:

1. *Do you know more about good study habits than your grades reflect?* Then why don't you get better grades?

2. *Do you know more about diet, correct eating habits, nutrition, and chemical intake than your body reflects?* I thought so.

3. *Do you know more about the importance of daily exercise programs than your physical condition currently reflects?* I see.

4. *Do you know more about the discipline it takes to maintain a quality devotional life than your current spiritual condition reflects?* Hmm.

If you are like most people, you probably answered *yes* to the above questions. Why, then, don't we use what we know? Why do we allow our mind's creative capacity to remain practically untapped? Are we that lazy? Perhaps a few of us are, but a far more familiar explanation for our ineptitude is fear, and especially, fear of failure.

In his excellent book *Seeds of Greatness* (Revell), Dr. Denis Waitley defines *fear* as "False Education Appearing Real" and says there are three dominant fears:

Fear of Rejection, which is being made a fool or failure in the sight or presence of others.

Fear of Change, which is charting unknown waters, being first, breaking tradition, sacrificing external security.

Fear of Success, which is an expression of guilt associated with our natural desire for self gratification.

These fears are like roadblocks in our brains, diverting the free flow of information. Fears associated with past failures are often the result of a false label tacked onto us when we were younger.

At ten years of age, Annie was shy and rather reluctant to ask questions in school, even if she didn't understand something. One night as her daddy was tucking her into bed, she mustered up the courage to tell him about her problem.

"Annie," he said reassuringly, "don't ever be afraid to ask questions in class. If you don't ask questions, how will you ever learn anything new?"

Bolstered a bit by her father's encouragement, Annie approached her teacher the following day during study hall.

"Miss Dikes," she whispered softly, so the other students could not hear.

"Yes, Annie?" Miss Dikes responded without looking up from the papers she was grading.

"Miss Dikes, I have some questions about the math problems you assigned this morning. Would you mind explaining how to do them once again?"

Miss Dikes disgustedly slammed her red pen onto the desk. She sat up straight in her chair, looked directly into Annie's eyes and said curtly and loudly, "How dense can you be?"

Humiliated, Annie didn't answer Miss Dikes's question. In fact, Annie never answered another of Miss Dikes's questions the entire school year. Prior to this, Annie had been an outstanding student in math. From this time on in her academic career, Annie would constantly struggle with the subject.

Years later, Annie admitted, "A lot of people said nice things about me when I was a child, but the only comment I can remember from elementary school is that awful condemnation from Miss Dikes."

Keep Expanding

Fear of failure can immobilize you unless you continually expand your knowledge and adjust your awareness. You can do this in two ways. One, as you acquire knowledge, condition your mind to accept only labels put on you that are consistent with the labels attached to you by your Designer. People can say all sorts of nasty things about you, but *you* decide what you are going to believe.

Second, view each failure as a learning experience, and turn your stumbling blocks into stepping-stones toward future accomplishments.

Thomas Edison, the indefatigable inventor who patented close to eleven hundred of his experiments, failed *ten thousand times* in his attempt to create a light bulb!

Was he wasting his time during those early endeavors? No way!

He could say, "I now know nine thousand, nine hundred and ninety-nine ways how *not* to make a light bulb." Thomas Edison would not allow himself to remain depressed over the failures he experienced as he expanded his knowledge. His motto was: "When things get you down, remember Jonah; he came out all right!"

You're not the first person to make a mistake; millions of people do it every day. The big difference between the failures and the fighters is that when a good fighter gets knocked down, he gets back on his feet and gets back in the ring.

So you've failed a time or two. Woody Allen, the famous film producer, *flunked* Motion Picture Production at the City College of New York. Leon Uris failed English three times in high school. He went on to write one of the most popular novels of this century, *Exodus*. Popular rock performer and television star Rick Springfield was so shy at sixteen years of age he played his guitar with his back turned toward the audience. Springfield turned things around, though, and went on to produce three platinum albums. "I believed that if I kept working my craft, I would be successful," said Springfield. "My happiness comes from proving to myself that perseverance pays off" (*Tiger Beat*, January 1986).

See if you recognize this fellow: He was the tenth of eighteen children. His father was a heavy boozer; his mother deserted when the boy was only five years old. Consequently, this young man grew up in a series of foster homes. Well, let's say he lived there occasionally. He ran away eight times before he was seven years of age.

He failed two years of school and eventually was put into a reform school to straighten up his life. He did, and he became one of the best known comedians of our time. When Flip Wilson flaunts his famous line, "What you see is what you get!" he may be more psychologically and theologically accurate than he knows.

What do *you* see? How do you see yourself? As you read on, I want you to keep these questions constantly in mind, because your answers will go a long way toward helping you to use the talent and knowledge you have acquired.

Talent and *knowledge* are important factors in all of our lives, but the most important ingredient that will influence how well we live up to our potential is *desire*. Let's see how desire can determine our destination, after your consider this chapter's Inside Out.

Inside Out for
"Potentially Yours"

1. List *five* attributes about yourself with which you are pleased.

2. List *five* areas that you want to work to develop.

3. How can you make better use of your Designer-given talents or abilities at school or at work?

4. If you could be someone else for a year of your life, who would it be and why?

5. We are not all knowledgeable in the same areas. Describe an area where you feel you are a budding expert.

6. Bob Geldof saw a need and moved to meet it. What needs do you see in people who live around you, and how can you help to meet them? (See Matthew 10:42.)

7. Read Luke 12:41–48. How does this passage relate to your talents?

8. Go to the library this week. Check out a book that will expand your horizons in a positive way.

A Streetcar Named *Desire*

One night after an ABRAHAM concert, a young man was wandering around the stage. I had noticed the fellow ogling the drums earlier in the day, when we had done an assembly program in his school. Now here he was again. Hoping to be an encouragement to him, I went over and initiated a conversation.

"Do you play?" I asked, as I nodded toward the drums.

"Oh, no!" he quickly responded. "I'd give anything if I could though, Ken. I'd love to be able to play like you."

"Hey, thanks for the compliment," I answered. "I really appreciate that, but it doesn't take *anything* in order to play. It just takes a little practice and a lot of patience as you learn. You could do it if you wanted, I'll bet."

"Oh, no! Not me!" he replied emphatically. "I could *never* learn to play these things. Why, you play the right cymbal with your right hand, the snare drum with your left hand, the bass drum with your right foot, and the hi-hat with your left foot . . ."

"Whoa! Whoa! Whoa!" I interrupted him. "I thought you said you could never learn! It sounds to me like you already have!"

"Well, I did take a few lessons," he muttered.

"And?"

"I quit."

"Why?"

"Aw, I just couldn't get the hang of these things," he picked up a pair of drum sticks as he replied.

"How long did you take lessons?" I asked.

"Mmm, about six weeks, I guess."

"Six weeks! That's hardly even getting started! You quit after six weeks? I thought you said you'd give *anything* to be able to play?"

"Well, not exactly *anything*," he replied with a sheepish grin. "I figured I'd give it a try and if I caught on, great! If I didn't pick it up quickly, I'd cash in my chips. I guess I just didn't have the desire."

In this "instant society" of ours, we have grown accustomed to immediate success stories. Guess what? It just doesn't happen that way. Most overnight success stories take years of hard work and determination to develop.

Whether you are aspiring to be a first-team athlete, an A student, or a missionary to Africa, the one characteristic that will pull you out of the pit and put you on the path to where you want to be is *desire*. You've got to want it! You must have that burning drive within, if you are ever going to do it.

This desire is a developed habit. It's not something that your Designer stuffed into your genes. You were not born with an innate desire or lack of it. You must *learn* to be motivated in the right direction and for the right reasons.

Neither is desire something that can be driven into you by someone else. Pep rallies are encouraging; contests are fun; sermons are inspirational and challenging, but none of these things will bring about lasting results unless desire begins to build from within you.

Incentives are helpful, and as Tom Peters and Bob Waterman, the authors of *In Search of Excellence* (Harper & Row) have taught us, hoopla and recognition awards can be used effectively to spur people on toward greatness. The only problem with external incentives is that the "law of diminishing returns" soon sets in, and the incentive must continually be increased to get the same type of results.

That's what has happened to a lot of lazy, spoiled-brat kids. Mom and Dad started them out on "Come here, little Dumpling. Clean up your room, and you can have a scoop of ice cream!"

Then what does it take? Two scoops!

Then what? A pizza!

What next? A Porsche!

Then what? A condo on the beach in Hawaii!

What Cranks Your Motor?

As Christians, we are motivated by the ultimate desire: to please Jesus Christ. The apostle Paul even went so far as to say "To me, to live is Christ . . ." (Philippians 1:21). Not that we serve an overbearing taskmaster who is happy with us only when we live perfect Christian lives. On the contrary. Jesus is the One person who truly knows us, and accepts us just the way we are, and forgives us completely when we repent of our sins. In spite of our failures and sinfulness, He loves us. He paid the price for our salvation and He is not going to give up on us now.

This knowledge spawns what Stuart Briscoe refers to as "The Gratitude Attitude" (Stuart Briscoe, tape series, *What Makes Christians Tick?* Telling the Truth, Inc.; Brookfield, WI). This is the idea: because our Designer has done so much for us, there wells up within us an overwhelming desire to do His will, enthusiastically and without concern for cost or sacrifice. Consequently, Christians should be some of the most motivated creatures on earth. Paul tells us, "And whatever you do in word or deed, do all in the name of the LORD Jesus, giving thanks through Him to God the Father" (Colossians 3:17).

Paul's advice gives us the pattern and the purpose of all Christian personal improvement programs. The pattern is to say and do everything as unto Christ; the purpose is to give thanks and glory back to our Creator.

The Apostle lived this way. He had developed the practice of moving toward the goals he had set in his life and ministry, and he would tolerate little or no distractions, apart from a direct revelation by the Holy Spirit. Even in the face of monumental problems and numerous delays and setbacks, Paul's inner drive, his gratitude attitude, kept him moving toward his goals. He said:

> Not that I have already obtained it, or have already become perfect, but I press on in order that I may lay hold of that for which also I was laid hold of by Christ Jesus. Brethren, I do not regard myself as having laid hold of it yet; but one thing I do: forgetting what lies behind and reaching forward to what lies ahead, I press on toward the goal for the prize of the upward call of God in Christ Jesus.
>
> Philippians 3:12–14

Obviously, Paul was a man with a purpose. He knew where he was going, and he felt his goal deserved his best efforts. Unfortunately, a lot of us are striving toward goals that are not worthy of one who is the recipient of Designer Genes. No wonder we can't get motivated or develop the necessary desire to do great things. We've set our sights far too low.

There is a famous story about an anonymous missionary who was the object of a major oil company's courtings. The company executives authorized their representatives to offer the missionary any sum of money within reason, just to procure his services.

Still the missionary refused. Finally, in desperation, the oil company representative wrote out a check, but left the amount blank.

"Here," he said as he pushed the check toward the missionary, "fill in any amount of salary that you want."

The missionary stepped back with surprise. "Oh, I'm terribly sorry," he explained. "It's not that your salary is too small. The *job* is not big enough!"

That missionary's desire to serve Jesus on the mission field superseded any success the secular field could offer him. If you want to develop your full potential, be sure your goal is worthy of you, and then go for it.

Unfortunately, a lot of Christians can't get too fired up about anything. They're just "resting in the Lord." They'd rather *let* things happen to them, than *make* things happen. They'd prefer to *react*, rather than *act*. All the while, they feel more "spiritual" because they are submitting to the will of God and trusting Jesus to work everything out for them. Then, when things don't go the way they had planned, they feel even more self-righteous because they are suffering or being persecuted for Christ.

What hogwash! What garbage! Understand: as Christians, we *do* rest in Jesus. His Word to us is, "Trust in the LORD with all your heart, and do not lean on your own understanding. In all your ways acknowledge Him, and He will make your paths straight" (Proverbs 3:5, 6). But He also says: "Even so faith, if it has no works, is dead, being by itself" (James 2:17).

Too often, we are more motivated by fear than we are by desire, love, or gratitude. Fear of hell, fear of sinning, fear of failing in our Christian lives, keeps more Christians bound for destruction than on the track toward life.

Unquestionably, fear is a strong motivator. It is very difficult, however, to motivate someone in a positive direction through the use of fear. In *Don't Bite the Apple 'Til You Check for Worms*, I wanted to prevent young people from making tragic mistakes in their lives through the trap of premarital sex. I also wanted to inspire them to live pure, holy lives in the realm of their sexuality. In order to do so, I pointed out such fear motivators as pregnancy, venereal disease, and guilt. However, I also presented the positive reasons for avoiding premarital sex.

Not long after the book was published, a young woman came into my office to talk with me. "I want to thank you for writing that book," she said. "I always knew the dangers of premarital sex, but that never stopped me from sleeping with my boyfriend. It wasn't until I realized that there are logical, positive reasons for doing things God's way that I was able to develop the desire to do right. I didn't just *stop* having sex; I *started* to live a pure life!"

Certainly, some fear motivation is valid and necessary. Where would we be if Mom and Dad hadn't warned us: "Don't go out in the street. You might get hit by a car." or "If you don't keep your hands away from the stove, I'm going to smack your fingers."

As a rule, though, fear motivation is a negative life-style. Fear becomes the great compeller; it forces you to do something. We frequently hear people who are motivated by fear using phrases such as: "I have to" or "I'm afraid I must . . ." rather than "I want to," or "I can."

"Hey, Jill! Are you going to the basketball game tonight?"

"No, I *have to* study for my calculus test."

No, she doesn't. Jill doesn't *have to* study. She can decide not to study, if she wants. Of course, if she does, she has also decided to flunk calculus. Nevertheless, you'd be amazed at the difference in Jill's performance and attitude if she developed a habit of answering questions like this:

"Hey, Jill! Are you going to the basketball game tonight?"

"No; it sounds like fun, and I'm sure it will be a great game, but I want to study for tomorrow's calculus test. I know I can do well, so I'm going to spend some time preparing."

Sounds crazy? Try it. You will be pleasantly surprised at the results.

Reshape Your Thinking

"Come on, Ken," I can hear you saying, "Do you seriously mean to tell me that changing a few little words here and there can alter my life?"

Yep! The Bible makes it clear that your attitudes and thoughts have an overwhelming influence upon the way you do things. "For as he thinks within himself, so he is . . ." (Proverbs 23:7). Your words are merely extensions of your thoughts. Psychologists have verified this biblical principle in everyday life. They have discovered that human beings will move consciously or unconsciously toward that which their thoughts dwell upon, whether victory or defeat, success or failure.

That's why the apostle Paul instructed us to think positively, rather than negatively. Paul said ". . . whatever is true, whatever is honorable, whatever is right, whatever is pure, whatever is lovely, whatever is of good repute, if there is any excellence and if anything worthy of praise, let your mind dwell on these things" (Philippians 4:8). Psychologists have discovered an interesting corollary to Paul's principle. Apparently our minds have great difficulty putting negative thoughts into positive actions. That's why it's hard to lose weight when you keep reminding yourself how you look like "Ten Ton Tilly."

A friend of mine had a magnetic pink pig on her refrigerator door, along with the oft-quoted THOSE WHO INDULGE BULGE!

She said, "I finally had to take that silly thing down! I wasn't getting any skinnier, and I noticed that my reflection in the bathroom mirror was beginning to look more and more like that pig on my refrigerator."

We move toward that which our thoughts and desires are currently dwelling upon. If you want to lose weight, you need to start seeing yourself as thin. Think of how great you are going to look next summer in your new bathing suit. Think of how much energy you have because of the weight *you have already lost* in your mind. Let your mind dwell on pictures of you in your newly renovated form, eating healthy foods in the right quantities, exercising, and feeling good about it.

"Mind games?" you ask. Maybe. Do they work? My wife, Angela, will attest to it.

When Angela was growing up, she "saw herself" as a "full-figured" woman. Doting relatives had convinced her of this through such well-intentioned but misguided remarks as, "My, honey! You certainly are going to be a big girl! Yessir! She's a big one, she is! Big boned. Large framed. Why, I think she's going to turn out to be taller than her mother!"

It just goes to show, you can't believe everything you hear—even when it comes from loving relatives. To this day, Angela is two inches shorter than her mother. She is nowhere near being "large framed" or "big boned." She wears sizes one to three, if that gives you a hint.

Nevertheless, at that point in her life, Angela *thought* of herself as a large woman and her body responded by turning those thoughts into twenty pounds of excess weight. Today, however, Angela is a trim 105 pounds. How did she do it? Through some specialty diet? No. By attending Weight Watchers? Nope. As helpful as those may be for some people, the turning point in Angela's life came when she began to "see" herself as the tiny, petite, small-framed woman she is.

With a bright purple crayon, she wrote the number 105 on a piece of paper and taped it to her mirror, where she would see it each morning as she was getting ready for school. That was the number of pounds she wanted to be, so that was the number she dwelled upon.

One day Angela's ten-year-old cousin saw the reminder on the mirror and began to laugh uncontrollably. "Is that what you think you're going to weigh?" she blurted out through her tears of laughter.

"That's right," answered Angela matter-of-factly.

"But you weigh almost 125 pounds!" the cousin chuckled.

Angela looked at herself in the mirror and resolutely replied, more to herself than to her cackling cousin, "I will weigh less tomorrow."

And she did! Within two months, Angela was down to 105 pounds, and she never regained the unnecessary weight. Of course, she dieted and worked out, performing the most difficult type of exercise—pushing herself away from the table and closing the refrigerator door. But the battle was won in her mind before it would be won on her waistline.

Success Comes in Cans!

Success in life, whether in the spiritual realm or in the natural, is not reserved for those with extraordinary gifts or talents. Neither is it assured by a high IQ, exceptional knowledge, or birth into a certain family. It is rarely dependent upon abilities or equipment. But it is almost always associated with drive, desire, persistence, patience, and perseverance.

As I was driving along an interstate highway, I saw a billboard advertising a local company that recycles cans. In bold letters it read: SUCCESS COMES IN CANS! I zoomed past the sign at about 55 miles per hour, but the message stayed with me: SUCCESS COMES IN CANS!

That's it. I thought. *That's the secret. Success comes in* cans, *not* can'ts. If we dwell upon what we can't do, we'll never do much of anything. If we believe that we *can* do something, God will help us to get it done, assuming, of course, that it is according to His plan, and will result in glory to His name.

When the band ABRAHAM first began, we didn't have a bass guitar player. One evening, after a practice session, we were praying that God would send us a bass player, and my younger brother, Tink, overheard us. (His real name is Howard George Abraham, Junior. That's why we've always called him *Tink*.)

He bounded into the room the instant the last "Amen" was said.

"I can do it!" he cried. "I know I can do it. Just give me a chance. I can play bass guitar!"

"Go on; get outta here," older brothers, John and I, responded virtually in unison.

"You're too young," continued John. "You're only twelve years old. Not only that, you don't even own a guitar."

"No, I don't," Tink persisted, "but my buddy, Brian, has one. I know he'd let me borrow it."

"But you've never *played* a guitar," I attempted to reason with Tink. "What makes you think you could play it, even if you had one?"

"I know I can do it. I know I can. The Lord will help me!"

"All right, all right," John pacified him. "You go learn to play guitar and come back to see us when you get it down pat."

"Okay!" Tink shrieked, as he raced out the door toward Brian's house. We all had a good laugh over his enthusiasm while we packed our sound equipment.

At the practice session the following week, Tink was back—with Brian's guitar.

"I'm ready!" he beamed, when he saw the other instruments being unpacked.

"Ready for what?" asked John.

"Well, you said to go learn to play, and then come back, so here I am, ready to play!" Tink held the guitar to his chest as he spoke. The instrument was several inches taller than he was, but he held it as if it were a feather duster.

"But you've never had any lessons," I protested.

"Don't need any," Tink quickly replied. "I taught myself."

"Why, you don't even know how to tune those things," John pointed to the strings on the guitar.

"Don't need to," Tink returned. "I just tune them to where I think they sound good, and play the right notes from there."

John rolled his eyes toward the ceiling.

"Come on, let's go!" Tink said excitedly, as he plugged the cheap guitar into a cheap amplifier. "We haven't got all night, you know."

"Okay, okay. Let's get it over with," said John. "Let's hear what you can do."

At that point, our twelve-year-old brother, who had never had a guitar lesson in his life, sat down and played every song in our repertoire—without a mistake. He's been with the band ever since.

About a year later, we needed a piano player. When Tink said, "I can do it," we believed him. Today, Tink plays nearly fifty thousand dollars worth of keyboard instruments during an ABRAHAM concert.

Success comes in *cans.*

Obviously, it takes more than mere optimism to live life to your fullest, Designer-given potential. It takes talent, knowledge, desire—and then some—to make your dreams come true. But when you believe that your Designer has created you for a purpose, that He wants the best for you, and you are motivated by a desire to serve Him in loving gratitude, the possibilities and opportunities are practically limitless.

Granted, a lot of talented and educated young people fail to utilize their gifts or reach their goals. Sometimes they simply lack that all-important *desire.* More often, though, the reason they cannot live up to their potential is due to the way they view themselves. Their self-esteem is so low, they are selling themselves short. Their self-image has been so beaten and battered, they have trouble seeing themselves as anything but losers.

If that sounds like you, stay with me! I have good news for you after this chapter's Inside Out.

Inside Out for
"A Streetcar Named *Desire*"

1. *Name some* have-tos *in your life. How can you change those to* I want tos? *For example: change "I have to go to school," to "I want to further my education."*

2. *What factors influence you the most in making your decisions?*

3. *Read Philippians 4:8. How does this verse relate to your drive and determination?*

4. *Name three negative habits you have formed that you want to change in the future. What are the obstacles that stand in your way? How can you best overcome those obstacles, beginning today?*

5. *Sylvester Stallone was turned down by nearly every major producer in Hollywood when he attempted to peddle his script. That script turned out to be the megablockbuster* Rocky. *Is there some project that you believe in, but nobody else does? Never give up! How can you best sell what you are doing?*

6. *Name three of the strongest motivators in your life right now. What are they influencing you to do?*

Who Do You Think You Are?

4

"Hey, Tina! Wanna go for a ride?"

Tina looked up from her Big Mac and saw Sam and Lucky stretched out on opposite sides of a booth across the room, right next to the life-sized cardboard image of Ronald McDonald.

For a moment, she could hardly suppress a smile as she thought, *The two of them, plus Ronald . . . they look like The Three Stooges! Sam, with his bowl-shaped haircut, and Lucky with his pot gut; Ronald, you really should be more careful about who you're hangin' out with!* The smile faded quickly as Tina glared at the sleazy leaches in the corner. She despised Sam, and could barely tolerate Lucky.

"Why would I want to go anywhere with you guys?" Tina answered quietly but sarcastically, her mouth still partially filled with food.

"Hey, Tina! 'Cause we love you, that's why!" Sam mocked. "Who loves you any more than we do, huh? Tell me!"

Hmph. He may have a point there, Tina mused. Her father divorced her mother when Tina was fourteen years old. He left. No good-byes. No alimony. Nothing. He just went out the door and never came back.

Not that Tina missed him. He and Tina had never gotten along anyhow. He swore at her all the time, and was constantly hassling her over the way she wore her hair, or how tight her jeans fit, or how low her necklines were. How did he say it? "Tina, you're too mature for your age. You're not a little girl anymore. You're a woman, and men will try to get everything they can off you!"

At night, he'd come home drunk, and from her bedroom Tina could hear him and Mom yelling at each other.

Tina never saw her father hit her Mom, but she heard the awful sounds, and saw the bruises on Mom's face the mornings following one of his drunken binges.

He wouldn't hit Tina. Not with his fists, anyhow. He pounded her with words. Tina cringed in pain, as she thought of the horrible names he called her. "Slut." "Illegitimate." "Whore." "You're only good for one thing!" he screamed at her again and again. "Naahh, you're no good for nothing!"

"Hey, Tina! You wanna go or not?" Sam's voice startled Tina out of her memories. She shook her long, straight hair as if she had just awakened from a deep sleep.

"Huh? Oh, er, yeah, I guess. Why not?" she said more to herself than to anyone else. Tina looked at the Timex on her wrist. Eight o'clock. *Mom will be in church for at least another hour,* she thought.

"Hey, Tina! Don't worry about the time," Lucky called. "We'll get you back before your old lady gets out of church. She won't even miss you!" Lucky and Sam let out hideous horselaughs.

They're probably right, she sighed sadly. *Mom's been a mess since Dad left, and those good religious folks don't care a lick for me.*

"Come on, Tina! Let's go!" Sam's body hovered over her now.

59

"Yeah, let's get a move on," Lucky said coarsely, as he put his huge hand under Tina's arm and began pulling her out of the seat. "I'm ready for some action tonight!"

Tina jerked her arm out of Lucky's hand and the action sent the remains of her Big Mac sailing across the table, scattering onto the floor. Tina looked at it in disgust. *What a mess.* she thought. *Just like me!* She didn't bother to pick it up.

"All right," she growled. "Let's go. Where's your car?"

Tina knew what was in store for her with these two creeps. She'd been down this road before. More mauling, more pawing. When they were done with her, they'd bring her back into town and dump her off someplace.

Aw, who cares, she told herself. *Dad doesn't. Mom is a religious recluse; she's not even able to handle her own problems. Why should I care about myself?* She opened the door and got into the backseat of Lucky's car.

I wish Tina was a fictitious character I simply made up for this story. She's not. She's a real person. Pathetically real. No, her name is not Tina, but she exists—if you can call her kind of life existing, that is.

Saddest of all, she is not alone. Thousands of young people throughout North America have been devastated by crippling low self-esteem. Their self-concepts, the images they have of themselves, have been so severely distorted, many of them may never fully recover.

What Is Self-Esteem?

With the new interest in self-awareness these days, it is easy to get confused over terminology. Is my self-esteem the same thing as my self-image? Do my self-image and self-esteem differ from my self-concept? How do I measure my self-worth?

No wonder we get confused! In my desk-top dictionary, I counted nearly four hundred different words and their derivatives dealing with the *self*. Descriptions for the self run the gamut from *self-abandonment* to *self-worship*. So do our personalities and life-styles.

Self-esteem, though, is that deep-down feeling you have about your own worth. It's how you regard yourself. It's your opinion or judgment of your own value, the extent to which you think you matter in this life. It's that feeling that says, "I like myself" or "I dislike myself."

Your *self-image* is much like a self-portrait of yourself. It is who and what you picture yourself to be.

Since most people are not clinical psychologists, the words *self-image, self-esteem, self-concept,* and *self-worth* are often used interchangeably, even though there are slight differentiations in actual meanings. For our purposes, that will do fine. Basically, we're talking about what you think of yourself. Who do you think you are?

So What's the Difference?

Unquestionably, a heathy self-image is one of the key factors in the success and happiness of any individual. The reason your self-concept is so important is: you will probably talk, act, and react like the person you *think* you are. Psychologists have proven that you will most consistently perform in a manner that is in harmony with the image you have of yourself. Oh, sure, even with a negative self-concept you may occasionally break out of the pattern and belt one out of the park, or ace the big test, or get a date with your dreamboat. Conversely, even those individuals with healthy self-images blow it from time to time. But usually, your mind will complete the picture you tell it to paint of yourself.

If you see yourself as ugly, unlovely, inferior, or inadequate, you will probably act in accordance with your thoughts. If your self-worth is low, you will imagine yourself as a born loser, a washout, a filthy, unforgiven sinner who is unworthy of God's love or anybody else's.

"I can never do anything right."
"Why me?"
"I'll never amount to anything."

These are just a few of the phrases that dominate the conversation of a person with poor self-esteem.

On the other hand, individuals who know they have been given Designer Genes are usually happy about who they are. They know that they have been created in the Designer's own image (Genesis 1:26, 27), and He has crowned them with honor (Psalms 8:4, 5). They feel good about themselves, because they have learned that their Designer loves them, and *He* feels good about them!

They can honestly say, "Thanks Lord, for creating me. I know You have a purpose for designing me the way You did, and I'm glad to be me. I'd rather be me than any other person on earth. You have promised that You are going to do something absolutely *supernatural* with my life."

Your Own Motion Picture

The self-image is not a physical part of your body. It is more a subconscious "governor," that controls your actions and performance. All of the positive thinking, motivational messages, goal-setting seminars, and coaching will be virtually useless to you if your self-image tells you that you are a failure!

Brent was scared stiff. It was the last of the ninth in the game that would decide the City Championship. The score was tied; the bases loaded, two outs . . . and Brent was walking from the on deck circle to the batter's box.

It's all up to me, he thought frantically to himself. *This is it! The entire year comes down to what I do in the next few seconds. Oh, me! What if I strike out?* he wondered, as the pitcher wound up to release a blazing fast ball.

"Steee—rike One!" the umpire roared.

Yikes! shrieked Brent's subconscious mind. *Only two more strikes and I'm out. We'll have lost the championship, and all because of me.*

Smack! The white sphere, traveling over ninety miles an hour, cracked into the catcher's mitt a second time. Brent's bat hung limply above his shoulder.

"Steee–rike Two!" bellowed the home-plate ump.

Oh, golly. Brent mulled. *This is it! This is my last chance. If I miss this one, it's over.* He gripped harder on the wooden bat.

"Whooosh!" The curve ball cut directly in front of Brent's belt, and the opposing team's fans erupted in jubilant celebration. Amid the din, Brent heard the umpire's piercing voice reverberate through the stadium, "Steee–rike Three! You're out!"

Three perfect opportunities to score and to win had passed him by, and Brent never even took a cut! Why? Because Brent's self-image told him he was a loser. Consequently, when he stepped up to the plate, rather than seeing himself as a hero, knocking the baseball into next week, he "saw" himself as striking out, which his subconscious mind promptly helped him to do.

Many Christian young adults fall into that same trap. They know that it is possible to live a fruitful, victorious Christian life, but they are afraid of failing, so they fail to step out in faith. They know other people who have overcome huge obstacles to do great things for God, but they can't imagine anything like that happening to them. They wallow in deep-seated inferiority complexes, feelings of inadequacy, and are tied up in knots by their own low self-worth.

Remember Moses

Have you ever felt like that? If so, don't despair. Remember Moses? God appeared to him through the burning bush and told Moses that he was the guy to deliver the people of Israel from the oppression of Pharaoh (Exodus 3:10). And what did Moses do? He went bananas.

He said, "But God! I'm just a nobody. Who am I, little nerd-head me, that I should go to the ruler of Egypt and lead the people out of his country?"

But God said, "No problem, Moses. *I* will be with you" (v. 12).

Wow! Talk about a heavy-duty calling card! Still Moses was feeling scared and inadequate. No doubt, he was visualizing a thousand catastrophes that were sure to happen under his leadership. His negative self-image would not allow him to envision success, even though he had received a definite call from God.

God was willing to be patient with Moses and work with him through all of his insecurities, inhibitions, and self-image problems. But Moses continued to voice his faithless fears: "What if they will not believe me, or listen to what I say? For they may say, 'The LORD has not appeared to you'" (Exodus 4:1). Moses was worried about being accepted by his peers. After all, they might reject him and not believe his word. Can you imagine if one of your old buddies suddenly showed up back in town after a long absence and said, "Okay, gang. I have been talking with God, and He told me that you guys are supposed to follow me!" Right!

Furthermore, Moses felt that somebody else (anybody else!) could probably do a much better job at this project than he would (4:13). Now Moses' fears were not totally unfounded. He knew that he wasn't a polished public speaker, and the idea of getting up in front of a large group of people didn't really thrill him a lot. You can understand that feeling, can't you? You know how those butterflies start reproducing in your stomach every time you have a report to give at school, or the pastor asks you to lead the youth group in prayer. Well, what if you knew you had to get up in front of *a million* people, most of whom didn't have the foggiest idea of who you were, and your speech had to convince these people that you were God's man (or woman) for the hour?

That's what God was asking Moses to do. No wonder Moses felt a little uncomfortable. No wonder he felt inadequate.

Nevertheless, Moses began to realize that the God of all creation was on his side, that he truly *was* God's man for the hour, and that the Master Planner had a plan for his life too. At that point, Moses' self-image began to change, his self-esteem started to rise, and he began to trust not simply in his own abilities and personality, but in the power of the Master Planner. If God said he could do it, then Moses believed that he would be *able to perform* whatever task necessary to get the Lord's work accomplished.

Have you ever felt that God was asking you to do something that you wouldn't feel comfortable doing, or capable of doing? Something that you knew you simply did not have the talent and ability to perform? Right at that point, your self-image may be at an all-time low.

The next time something like that comes along, and you're tempted to think that there is no way you can ever succeed, remember Moses. God was with him and helped him every step of the way, despite his failures and feelings of inadequacy. When Moses began to realize that the God of all creation was on his side, amazing and miraculous events began to happen in his life.

Similarly, your Designer has promised to be with you. Allow Him to change your self-image into His original design for you, and then, watch out! He has great things in store for your future.

Inside Out for
"Who Do You Think You Are?"

1. What elements in Tina's story sound a lot like your life?

2. Explain the difference between anonymous and unnecessary. Which term more closely describes your life?

3. Read 1 Corinthians 12:12–26. Where do you fit into Christ's "body"?

4. Tell how you would describe yourself over the phone to a potential blind date.

5. How would this description differ from your Designer's description of you?

6. Place on a table a penny, a nickel, a dime, a quarter, and a dollar bill. Using these standards of value, which one would best describe your life? Why?

7. If Hollywood made a movie of your life, and you were the star, what would the title be?

8. Describe a time when you felt inadequate for what the Lord wanted you to do. How did your responses compare with Moses' (Exodus 3, 4)?

9. How would you describe the self-images of Lee Iacocca? Ronald Reagan, Robert Schuller, Dan Marino? Jimmy Swaggart? Ernest Angsley?

Self-Worth versus Self-Worship

One of Satan's most subtle strategies has been to distort or destroy the self-images of Christian young people. The devil knows that you will perform in accordance with your own picture of yourself; if he can sow a negative self-concept within you, it won't be long before you will respond with corresponding negative conduct.

Until recently, very few Christians attempted to thwart Satan's devious designs in this area, let alone stage a counterattack. Fortunately, many parents, teachers, pastors, Christian psychologists, and youth workers are now attempting to provide young people with positive input, principles to help them develop a sound, biblical self-image.

The apparent negligence of the past existed largely because many Christians felt reluctant to acknowledge the value of ideas reflecting self-worth, self-image, and self-acceptance. Furthermore, the whole field of psychology, and especially "Christian Psychology," has been scrutinized with sincere suspicion by a large portion of the Christian community. The so-called truly devout have often looked with disdain upon such ideas as self-improvement, motivation, planning, and even goal setting.

Some of these concerns are warranted. Today, we are being inundated by a raft of narcissistic literature extolling the merits of self-awareness, self-confidence, and self-adulation. Books like *Pulling Your Own Strings, Loving Each Other, The Road Less Traveled, Think and Grow Rich,* and others like them have had an enormously wide influence. Coupled with the pronounced increase of prosperity preaching and success teaching, both within and outside of the Church, many cautious Christians are warning that it is only a matter of time before the seething pot of selfishness pours out into society. Many believe the soup has already been spilled.

Of even greater concern, cautions a wary William Kirk Kilpatrick, is how the current "pop" psychology tends to undercut the Gospel message. Kilpatrick explains in an interview with Ivan Thorn in the December 1984 issue of *HIS* magazine:

> Psychology says we should accept ourselves as we are: "We're okay the way we are and we only need to learn how to be ourselves." Christianity, on the other hand, says, "There is something wrong with us the way we are, and we need a transformation before we start patting ourselves on the back." If psychology is right about this, it reduces the good news of the gospels to the status of "nice" news—nice because there was never anything wrong with us. And all this business about needing a savior is rendered superfluous . . . If we are not sinners in need of a savior, then Christianity loses its point.

Other Christians are dismayed that an unbalanced emphasis upon self-love will breed a burgeoning population of young people who are addicted to self-pride. I must admit that for this reason the first time I heard a message on loving myself, preached by a classy, conservative youth evangelist, I tuned him out completely. His words smacked too much of pride to me, and I had learned well that "Pride goes before destruction ..." (Proverbs 16:18). Moreover, I knew that God was opposed to the proud person (1 Peter 5:5), and I didn't want Him to be opposed to me!

Looking back, I now see that the evangelist was right on target; I was the one who had been misguided. Having a high opinion of yourself, a positive self-image, is not necessarily the same as pride. Conversely, having low self-esteem does not mean you are a humble person. Some of the most arrogant people I've met have had lousy self-images, and some of the most humble folks have had valid, positive self-concepts.

In *His Image ... My Image* (Here's Life Publishers), Josh McDowell, draws a much-needed distinction between a positive sense of self-worth and the sin of pride. "*Self-worth* is a conviction that you have fundamental value because Jesus died for your sins. *Pride* points to self. It is rooted in the pleasure you find in yourself for what you believe you can do or have done with your life. Pride is an attitude of superiority, a puffed-up mentality, that manifests itself in an arrogant, unrealistic estimation of oneself in relation to others."

Ever since Adam and Eve first blew it in the Garden of Eden, human beings have been erring toward one extreme or the other regarding our opinions of ourselves. Sometimes, we tend to think more highly of ourselves than we should, leaning toward sinful pride. We feel, as did Adam and Eve, that *we* should be like God. *We* want to decide which of His commands we will obey and which we will ignore. *We* want to decide what is right and what is wrong. *We* want to call the shots in our lives—to do our own thing—rather than what God wants us to do.

This attitude, of course, is the very essence of sin. It is rooted in an exalted view of self, and it was the cause of rebellion in the lives of Adam and Eve. This, in turn, was the cause of their downfall and ultimate rejection from the Garden.

On the other hand, we sometimes tend to wallow in the quagmire of low self-esteem. Because we know we are "fallen creatures," we think of ourselves as worthless. We look down upon ourselves; some people even hate themselves. We know that we have sinned, so we despise ourselves as fallen failures. Like Adam and Eve, we feel ashamed, naked, and fear being exposed.

Both of these extremes are aberrations from what our Designer originally intended. We must come to understand that although we may be marred, sullied, torn, or tattered, the One who created us with Designer Genes is not content to cast us aside without offering every possible opportunity to be cleansed, renewed, and restored. At the same time, we need to face the truth that when we sin, we *ought* to feel awful! If you have violated someone else, or yourself, or God's standards, it is not surprising that you don't feel good about who you are. You don't need to "accept yourself"; you need to repent and make things right.

Balancing these two potentially explosive elements of self-image, pride versus healthy self-esteem, on the tightrope of daily Christian living is such a delicate matter, many believers are afraid to attempt it. If you fall off the straight and narrow way in either direction, you are condemning yourself to destruction. "Better, perhaps," some Christians say, "to simply stay off the rope."

Worm-ology

Unfortunately, for many of the Baby Boomer Generation and their children, it is already too late. The plunge has been taken by default. Many modern-day Christians have grown up under what is "affectionately" referred to as *worm theology*. Worm theology is that view of Christianity in which we are considered to be nothing more than insignificant worms; slithering, ugly, sinful creatures who are worthy only to be squashed underfoot, and then pitched into the fires of hell. This was the first impression I received regarding the subject of self-image, following my conversion to Christianity. It didn't take me long to discover that the "only acceptable self" was a "dead self." As a new believer, who had no comprehension of what the apostle Paul meant by being "crucified with Christ" (Galatians 2:20), I figured being a worm was as good as being dead. I'd just wait for God to step on me with a Monty Python sort of shoe!

Even the music seemed to support this strange, slippery theology. Two of my early favorites that I learned to sing as a believer were "At the Cross" and "Amazing Grace," both beautiful classics, but both strong conveyors of worm theology, if not properly interpreted.

"At the Cross" says:

> *Alas! and did my Savior bleed,*
> *And did my Sovereign die*
> *Would He devote that sacred head*
> *For* such a worm as I.
>
> ISAAC WATTS (emphasis mine)

See what I mean? Worm theology! And my new-believer's anthem, "Amazing Grace" didn't do much to change my thinking.

> *Amazing Grace how sweet the sound*
> *That saved a* wretch like me.
>
> JOHN NEWTON (emphasis mine)

I couldn't figure that one. Just a few days ago I was a popular, successful, senior in high school. Then, I met the Creator of the Universe; now, suddenly, I was nothing but a worm and a wretch? It didn't make any sense! Thankfully, I was too caught up in the joy of my newfound relationship with Christ to worry about worms and wretches. The benefits of becoming

71

a Christian far overshadowed any theological inconsistencies I may have noticed at the time.

Of course, apart from Jesus, we *are* worms and wretches. There is no limit to how low a person can sink, if he or she chooses to worship the creation rather than the Creator (*see* Romans 1). Nevertheless, once we trust Jesus as our Savior, we become brand-new creatures. The old things are passed away, new things have come (2 Corinthians 5:17).

Phil Driscoll dynamically reminded me of this truth. When I first met Phil, we were performing on the same program at the Civic Arena in Pittsburgh for a special evening of praise and prayer on behalf of the city's unemployed. All I knew about Phil was that before committing his life to the Lord, he had played for Joe Cocker on the rock 'n' roll circuit. I had never heard Phil Driscoll play a trumpet, and I was beginning to feel slightly sorry for him. *After all,* I thought, *what is one guy with a trumpet going to do in this huge arena?*

I needn't have worried. Phil Driscoll walked calmly onto the platform and began to play "Amazing Grace"—unlike any rendition of the song I had ever heard! Ten thousand people in Pittsburgh's Civic Arena sat enraptured as Phil's lilting strains of "Amazing Grace" vibrated the building.

The surprise came when Phil began to sing the words to "Amazing Grace." Instead of singing the standard lyrics "a wretch like me," he changed them to "a soul like me." Later, Phil commented, "I once *was* a wretch without Jesus, but not anymore. Now, I've been transformed. It's a new me!" I had to smile as I listened to Phil. Secretly, I was wondering what he could do with "At the Cross"!

Eating Humble Pie

Humble pie tastes awful, especially when it is laced with pride. Yet many Christians continue to chew the stuff, despite the knowledge that their Designer has disclaimed the unpalatable mush. Why would they do such a silly thing? Because they have a confused concept of humility.

Genuine humility is one of the grandest virtues a person can have. Too bad, some people have substituted an attitude of self-belittling and self-abnegation for the positive, holy trait of godly humility.

You know this sort of person. He or she goes around constantly dredging themselves through the dirt, always putting himself or herself down. They live with the mistaken notion that they are being "lowly." "Be a doormat for Jesus!" is their motto, along with Rodney Dangerfield's famous remark, "I don't get no respect." Such negativism would be bad enough in itself, but when Christians "spiritualize" their negative words and attitudes about themselves, thinking they are demonstrating how humble they are, their self-deprecation becomes an insult to God!

"I guess God loves me, but I sure can't stand myself."
"Oh, what a klutz!"
"I'm good for nothing."
"I can never do anything right."
"Everything I touch, I mess up."
"What a rotten person I am."
"God could never use my life."

The truth is, these personal put-downs are *not* characteristic of genuine, godly humility. In fact, this sort of talk about ourselves runs counter to everything our Designer has said about us. Christian humility means that we are able to live without the incessant need to attract attention to ourselves. While we recognize our sinfulness, we refuse to dwell upon it. Rather, we choose to concentrate on Christ, who He is, and who *we* are in Him. Honest humility acknowledges our strengths as well as our weaknesses, our failures as well as our successes. We don't need to get puffed up over our successes; nor do we need to flagellate ourselves for our failures. In good times and bad, we are trusting in our Designer who has promised to use all things that come to us for His glory and for our good (Romans 8:28).

73

Poor, Poor, Pitiful Me!

Some people confuse feeling sorry for themselves with true humility. Others, who feel emotionally hurt, rejected, damaged, or defensive, may think they are humble, when, in fact, their pseudohumility is only a thin veneer for self-righteousness and pride. Their low self-image makes it almost impossible for them to be taught, corrected, or to receive constructive criticism.

Though no one at First Baptist Church would have suspected, Robert took excessive pride in his position as leader of his church youth group. He often talked in muted tones of "the Lord's leading," and "his special ministry." He employed a quiet, soft demeanor that lent credence to his humility and hid the true motivation behind his feigned service. He was determined to be a great youth leader, so he poured himself into the work. Unfortunately, it was obvious to everyone except Robert that he was still a pupil and not a teacher.

When the youth advisor kindly asked him to give up his position and take a role of lesser responsibility in the church, Robert's self-righteous pride surfaced, and he put up a furious fuss. He took each word that had been spoken in love, and twisted it until it became a barbed, personal criticism and rebuke. Robert would not accept the youth advisor's gentle efforts to help him serve more effectively, and he left the church in a huff. His low self-esteem would not allow him to accept criticism.

On the other hand, some Christians find it equally as difficult to accept a compliment. When someone gives them a word of praise, their self-image says, "No, you cannot accept that. They must be talking about someone else. You don't deserve that compliment." Or, perhaps their self-image responds, "Watch out! It might be a trick. That person wouldn't say something nice about you for nothing. He must want something. They are going to deceive you, use you, or mistreat you some way."

Consequently, the person with a self-image problem will answer compliments with an "Aw, shucks. It was nothin'" attitude. "Everybody gets lucky once in a while." Or "I'll bet I couldn't do that again in a million years!"

When someone hands you some praise-on-a-platter, accept it graciously, and simply say, "Thank you." That's *it*. That is all the response necessary. You *don't* need to spend the next two hours belittling yourself, apologizing for your success, or rationalizing your choices. A simple *thank you* is all that is required.

Other Christians make a habit of "spiritualizing" their performances by attributing everything to Jesus. This, too, can be an indication of low self-esteem. One night, after ABRAHAM had done a concert with several artists, I passed one of Christian music's premier performers downstairs in the hallway leading to the dressing rooms. "Hey, great job tonight!" I complimented him as we passed. "You were absolutely super!"

He stopped cold, whirled around on the balls of his feet, as if I had lassoed him, and glared at me suspiciously. For a moment, I thought I had offended him. Then he answered in a hushed voice, "Hey, man. It wasn't me out on that stage tonight. It was Jesus."

I knew what he meant, but I decided not to resist being a bit mischievous and replied in my best ethereal tone, "Oh, wow, man! *Jesus!* That's really outta sight. I thought sure I saw *you* out on that stage tonight." He muttered something about the size of drummers' brains, as he clicked his heels together and continued on his way.

Of course we understand that as Spirit-filled Christians, it is "Christ in us" who does the work (Colossians 1:27). We know that we are dependent upon His Holy Spirit if anything of lasting eternal value is to be done. Nevertheless, He still does His work *through you*. Don't get cocky about it; He used a donkey one time too, remember. Conversely, you don't need to put yourself down every time someone gives you a word of encouragement for a job well done.

If you attempt to steal God's glory by bringing the attention to yourself, He will be quick to let you know it. This is pride, and you should rightfully repent of it. If, however, you are simply insecure about your self-image, and you attempt to remedy it by repeatedly repenting of pride, you are only magnifying your guilt and sealing your own tomb. You need to reconstruct your self-image and establish a proper sense of humility. This involves an honest assessment of your strengths and weaknesses (Romans 12:3), a willingness to consider others before yourself (Philippians 2:3), and the awareness that your talents and gifts come from your Designer for you to use in His service (1 Corinthians 4:7).

Genuine, godly humility seeks to serve other people as an expression of your love and commitment to Christ. It will turn your attention toward meeting *their* needs.

Whiners and Blowhards

Whiners and blowhards are not secure enough in their self-esteem to be able to do this. The whiners are always putting themselves down; the blowhards are always boosting themselves up. Both are desperately trying to prove their self-worth.

Wanda is a whiner. Though she is an excellent musician and vocalist, her self-image is such that she negates every performance. "Did I do okay? Did you hear that flat note I hit? I can't believe how badly I butchered that solo."

What is she doing? She is subtly seeking to hear words of praise that will prove to her that she did a good job. She craves compliments and flattery; she thrives on the stuff. She's waiting to hear "No, Wanda! I didn't notice the mistakes. You were fantastic! That solo was the best I've ever heard."

That's what Wanda really wants someone to say. But she is hampered by a sense of false humility, and her self-esteem is so low, she wouldn't dare ask for an honest appraisal. She would be shattered if someone ever told her, "Wanda, that solo really stinks!" Consequently, Wanda does the next best thing. She hangs negative statements about herself out on the line, hoping all the while that someone will come along and contradict her! Usually, nobody does.

On the other end of the spectrum is Barry the Blowhard. Barry *knows* he's good. In fact, in Barry's mind, he's the *best!* Not just the best in town, he's the best *ever.*

Barry has an insatiable need to be right. No, not once in a while; Barry has to be right all the time, in *every* situation. One thing you can count on about Barry, if you ask him a question, he will always give you a thorough answer—even if he doesn't understand the question! If he doesn't know the correct answer, he'll make one up. The words *I don't know, I'm sorry,* and *I was wrong* sound like phrases from a foreign language to Barry.

If you go into a restaurant with Barry, be prepared to duck. Barry's bombastic barrages will be flying everywhere. Insulting the waiters or waitresses, complaining about the food or the service, speaking with excessive volume or in crude language, as he tells you about the new job he is about to get, or his new car, or his new girlfriend (who just happens to be *the* most beautiful woman in the world!)—these are but a few of Barry's blundering attempts to tell you (and himself) who he is.

Barry's wardrobe looks like a billboard for Bloomingdales. If, perchance, he should buy something that does not have a designer's label on it, Barry will have it monogrammed with his own initials. Like many others who have bought the American Dream, Barry attempts to buy friends and personal esteem. He doesn't realize that his tendency to show off his many toys and possessions actually reveals his low opinion of himself, and his utter lack of confidence in himself apart from his accompanying accoutrements.

Both Wanda and Barry suffer from low self-esteem, yet both of them are extremely self-centered. They constantly are looking at, thinking about, or somehow attempting to draw the attention of others to *themselves.* Their whines and ballyhoo are actually cries of: "Help! I need attention. Please look at me!"

Sadly, because of their poor self images, Wanda and Barry seem to alienate the same people who would probably love them and accept them for who they really are, if given half a chance.

Individuals who are aware that they have been given Designer Genes usually have a healthy respect for the Designer and a healthy regard for themselves. They don't need to flaunt expensive toys or trinkets. If they achieve a measure of success, they can afford to be modest about it, because their self-esteem does not depend upon being a winner in this world. Their self-esteem is based in the source of all truly lasting success, Jesus Christ.

Inside Out for
"Self-Worth versus Self-Worship"

1. *Do you feel that God is for you or against you? Why?*

2. *Describe how you see the balance between self-worth and self-worship.*

3. *In your opinion, what does it mean to be a humble person. Describe someone you know who fits your definition.*

4. *Automaker John DeLorean was quoted in Life magazine (January 1986) as saying, "I was a pretty sick and strange guy. I was arrogant beyond belief, so arrogant, I believed I had humility." What do you suppose he meant by that? How could conceit be a symptom of a poor self-image?*

5. *How do you usually receive criticism? compliments?*

6. *Read Psalms 139:13–16. How does this passage relate to your estimation of yourself?*

7. *Can you find any "worms" in your theology? Describe God's opinion of your status in His Kingdom.*

8. *Think of someone you don't enjoy being around. Why don't you like this person? How is this person special to your Designer?*

9. *Is there someone you know who seems to feel unappreciated? Determine two ways you can help that person to realize he or she is significant.*

Mirror, Mirror on the Wall . . .

6

You weren't born with a particular self-image. Even though you were designed in the image of God, your own self-concept had to be developed and acquired. Where did it come from? How was your self-image formed, and what factors had the largest influence?

Two of the main sources of your self-image were your parents and your peers.

Certainly, your parents exerted a tremendous amount of influence over you from the time of your birth, on into your teens, and perhaps, beyond. They became the mirror in which you saw yourself reflected. Your family revealed their attitudes toward you by what they said to and about you, and of course, how they treated you. Soon, how they responded to you became what you believed to be true about you.

For example, if your parents constantly emphasized that you were a good boy, you began to think of yourself as a good boy. If your parents laughed at your jokes, you thought you were funny. If they listened when you wanted to talk with them, you gained the idea that you were a priority to Mom and Dad, and that your opinions had merit. Conversely, if you were told that you were stupid, or lazy, or clumsy, or shy, or loud, or fat, you adopted that self-concept and probably view yourself that way today, unless something has happened in your life to change that image.

Obviously, not all of the input we received from our parents was positive. Some of their mirrors were cracked or warped, or otherwise misshapen, which caused a distorted image to be reflected.

I'll never forget the first time I went to Idlewild Amusement Park and saw the huge concave and convex mirrors. In one, I looked like the Goodyear Blimp. In another, I was tall, lanky, and looked to be about six inches wide. Other mirrors distorted parts of my image, while allowing portions of my body to remain "normal." Have you ever tried to comb your hair in one of those things? If you're not careful, you may end up either combing your back or the hair of the guy standing next to you.

Although I had a lot of laughs while looking in those contoured mirrors, I was certainly relieved when I got home and could see an accurate image of myself in one of our family mirrors. But what if we had not owned a normal mirror, or all of our mirrors had been cracked or warped? The only image I would have known of myself would have been the cracked or warped picture in our family mirrors or the grossly twisted and distorted reflections I had seen at the park.

Parental Input

Similarly, many of the images we have seen or sensed being reflected by our parents and other family members have not always been fair or accurate. Some of them have been cruelly contorted. Take Marcy, for example.

Marcy's mother made a habit of correcting Marcy in public, right in front of the child's friends. If Marcy misbehaved in church, her mother would yank her to the rear of the sanctuary while the service was in progress, spank her indiscreetly, and then immediately march Marcy back up the center aisle, past the knowing snickers and smirks of the congregation.

"If nothing else, I'll embarrass her into being good," she often told Marcy's father.

Marcy's mom held back no fury when it came to berating her daughter. "You dummy! You idiot!" she would shout, regardless of who else heard. "How can you be so ignorant?"

As Marcy grew up, she not only accepted her mother's remarks; she *became* the person her mother told her she was—stupid, foolish, and ignorant. She fumbled through high school, entered college, and—predictably—flunked out. Mom shook her head as if to say, "See, I told you so!"

Because of Marcy's naive acceptance of whatever was told to her, family and friends soon dubbed her with such dubious distinctions as "Airhead" and "Space Cadet." Marcy's self-image responded with actions she felt were appropriate for an airhead, even though she was extremely intelligent and had good common sense.

After several more career failures, Marcy attempted to start her own business. She had always loved flower arranging, so she opened a small greenhouse. Almost overnight, she was wildly successful, and her greenhouse gave birth to a chain of flower shops. Monetary success and commensurate social prestige have followed Marcy ever since.

Oddly, Marcy remains frustrated, insecure, and suffers intense feelings of inadequacy. Despite her phenomenal financial and creative success, she still believes she is a failure. Why? Because a long time ago, her mother told Marcy that she was dumb, stupid, and ignorant. The young woman has never been able to shake that image.

Please understand: it is not that parents consciously and intentionally *try* to inflict negative self-concepts upon their children. On the contrary, most moms and dads do the best jobs they are capable of doing when it comes to the difficult challenge of raising positive kids in a grossly negative world. Many times they honestly don't realize that in their attempts to discipline bad behavior, they have unintentionally transferred the attitude that "you are a bad person." Psychologists and theologians agree, there must be a differentiation between behavior and the person. What is necessary is the "hate the sin, but love the sinner" attitude. Unfortunately, your folks may still be struggling with a few self-image hang-ups they inherited from *their* parents. Please be patient; God isn't finished with your parents yet, either!

Nor are you justified in blaming your parents for all of your inadequacies and failures. Ever since Adam and Eve, children have been impacted both positively and negatively by their parents. How we respond to that input makes the difference. Still, it is helpful to realize the important role your parents played in the development of your self-image.

If a child feels unacceptable to his or her parents, you can be sure that individual will find it necessary to overcome gargantuan self-image problems before he or she can feel loved and accepted by anyone else—even to be loved and accepted by God! Granted, imperfect parenting is not an insurmountable obstacle. If you have been the victim of misguided motivation, you simply must work harder at reconstructing a positive self-image. But, be encouraged! You need not live any longer in condemnation because of the past mistakes of your parents. It may take some time and study to redevelop your self-esteem, but with your Designer's help, you can do it. The fact that you have read this far in your attempt to discover how you can be a Designer Genes person is a clear indication that you are moving in the right direction.

Peer Pressure

A second source that greatly influenced the formation of your self-image has been your peer group.

The impact that your friends, classmates, boyfriends, and girlfriends have had upon your personality, either positively or negatively, has been incredible. How you dress, how you comb your hair, how you talk, and most important of all, how you view yourself has been influenced by the crowd with which you most often brush shoulders.

Sometimes our friends can be cruel.

In seventh grade, I was on the junior-high basketball team. One afternoon, I raced into the locker room and hurriedly began suiting up for practice. I was breathing rather heavily as I leaned over my buddy, Jack, and reached for my sneakers.

"Oh, man!" Jack barked. "Haven't you ever heard about mouthwash, Ken? Your breath smells awful!"

I joked with Jack, saying something about the onions on our hamburgers at lunch that afternoon, but the damage had been done.

For the next six months, my parents should have purchased stock in the companies that manufactured Scope, Certs, and Listerine. I was obsessed with the idea that I had bad breath. I became a halitosis hypochondriac. It took months of consistent reassurances by friends and family before I finally quit blowing my breath into my hand and sniffing for foul aromas.

Put-downs from your peers can be devastating, whether or not they are accurate portrayals of who you are. Negative comments from your peers sear right to the heart of your self-image. Unless you are abnormal, you have probably experienced ridicule for something. Maybe you are too fat, too small, too skinny, or have buck teeth, or "four-eyes." Perhaps you have been teased because your body is underdeveloped or overdeveloped, compared to the other kids; your voice is higher or lower than the rest of the gang, or perhaps your complexion is poor, or your teeth are crooked. If you have any deficiency at all, you can be sure that your peer group will find it, and will attempt to use it to drive your self-image through the basement floor.

Of course, it's *possible* for peer pressure to be a positive factor in shaping your self-image. It is, unfortunately, a rare and beautiful thing when our peers actually encourage us and enhance our self-esteem, especially during our younger days. The unwritten law of our junior years seems to be "Go for the jugular!"

Amy Grant has often confessed in concert that her early self-image was severely strained because of her "widow's peak," a strange, hereditary pointing of the hair on the top, front part of her head. While most of the other kids in her class were wearing their hair in long, straight styles, Amy lamented because hers kept curling over her forehead. Today Amy and her curls are famous, but back then, she was just as frustrated as you may be over some real or imagined quirk in your personality or appearance.

Three attitudes about yourself are susceptible to negative or positive input from parents and peers: (1) the *appearance* you believe; (2) the *accomplishments* you achieve; (3) the *attention* you receive.

The Appearance You Believe

In twentieth-century America, we are obsessed with how we look. The fashion designers, who have foisted their designer products upon us, know that we will pay almost any price in order to look good. Teenagers, especially, are prone to having their pockets plundered by the image makers. "Last year, America's 29.2 million teenagers spent $30 billion of their own money, much of it on clothing," according to Grady Hauser, vice-president for marketing of Teen-Agers Research Unlimited (Sara Rimer, "Teen-Agers Ever Seeking New Look," *The New York Times*, October 17, 1985).

Thirty billion dollars! Add to that the millions of dollars we spend every year on health and beauty aids, fitness programs, vitamins, makeup, cologne, and perfume—all in the often-vain attempt to improve our appearances. Then, if you still are not pleased with how you look, you can have cosmetic surgery to bend, trim, tuck, pin, pull, smooth out, or bypass whatever you have left.

Notice, though, that it is not how you actually look that figures most significantly in determining your self-esteem. It is how you *think* you look that counts. If you believe that you are a good-looking, attractive dresser, with a pleasing personality, you will most likely act that way. On the other hand, if you think of yourself as ugly, dumb, and unattractive, your self-image will cause you to fulfill your own prophecy.

Carly thinks of herself as being too tall. She *is* a bit taller than average, but she is a gorgeous young woman who could probably have a successful career as a fashion model. Too bad she has condemned herself to obscurity because of her attitude. When she was younger, her friends called her "beanpole," and the tag got stuck in Carly's image of herself. Now, she has gotten into the habit of walking with hunched shoulders, in a slightly slumped-over posture. She won't stand erectly for fear that she will tower over the fellows. She *believes* that she is unattractive, and for that reason, she is! If she would straighten up her self-image, she could straighten up her posture. She could then stand tall as the beautiful creature her Designer desires her to be.

The Accomplishments You Achieve

Next, after your personal appearance, few things will affect how you feel about yourself more than your personal accomplishments. "How am I doing?" or "How did I do?" are questions we constantly ask ourselves. We live in an intensely competitive and performance-oriented society. We know that nobody hangs around the loser's locker room. As such, there is a tremendous temptation to equate your self-worth with success or failure. In this regard, we are especially conscious of the approval or disapproval of our friends and family. Be careful, though: your self-esteem may be standing on slippery turf if it is tied to your performance.

After all, the same performance may bring approval from one source and disdain from another. Getting good grades, for example, may get you into good graces with your parents, while at the same time, your friends may despise you for blowing the class grading curve!

Some people base their self-esteem on how well they do in athletics or academics. Some derive their self-worth from their musical abilities, or their ability to amuse their friends, their sexual prowess, their ability to make money, get dates, or something else they can *do*. Of course, when they can no longer perform, or if someone else comes along who can do the same things equally as well, or better, then the doer's self-image is threatened, and oftentimes deflates like a punctured balloon.

Many Christians carry this attitude into their relationship with Christ. They feel that they must "perform" for God, like a puppet dangling on a string. They must earn His favor; they must show the Designer that His creation is worthy of love. As a result, they pour themselves into a works-oriented type of salvation, overemphasizing their works, and underestimating the value of faith, God's mercy, and His grace.

Cathlene is working herself into a frazzle in her attempts to prove to God, herself, and to the other people in town, that she is a good Christian. She is overextended in community events, politics, sports, and her church youth group. She bustles from one activity to the next.

Beneath her industrious exterior, however, is a little girl who is deathly afraid that if she ever ceases to perform for her daddy, he will withdraw his love, and the family members will disapprove of her as well. This childhood fear has now been transferred to Cathlene's heavenly Father, and the family of God. Cathlene desperately needs to discover that God has given her Designer Genes, and her worth is not dependent upon what she does for God.

The Attention You Receive

The attention you receive in life is directly proportional to how important you are in this world—at least, that's the message most of our self-images have interpreted. Attention equals status, to our way of thinking.

We've all seen the various award shows in which the stars make their grand entrances. Maybe you have dreamed, *I wish that could be me. Oh! For just a moment to bask in all that attention. The press of the crowd. The accolades of my peers. The adoration of the world. What I wouldn't give for a slice of that life!*

As amazing as it may sound, many people who have reached that status still regard themselves as failures. They are constantly worried about what other people are saying about them, and their fame is as fleeting as yesterday's newspaper reviews.

The late John Belushi may be the classic example of this in our times. Belushi grew up in Wheaton, Illinois, ironically, a haven for evangelical Christians. He began his career with Chicago's famous comedy troupe "Second City," and worked his way up to NBC-TV's "Saturday Night Live." There John Belushi became almost a cult hero, known for his zany, off-the-wall style of comedy. He made seven movies, and was wildly successful by the world's standards. Unfortunately, John Belushi seemed bent on killing himself with drugs. On March 5, 1982, in a bungalow just off Sunset Boulevard in Hollywood, he succeeded.

If you base your self-esteem on any of these conditional and transitory factors—what you look like, how well you peform, or how important you are in the eyes of the world—you are priming yourself for a large letdown. Certainly, these elements each play a part in the formation of your self-image, but don't exaggerate their importance.

Instead, take your self-concept from what your Designer has said about you. He created you. He knows what makes you tick. He knows your true worth; He bought and paid for you with the ultimate exchange. He gave His Son, Jesus, in exchange for you. That's how much value you have in the eyes of God.

All the gold in Fort Knox could not have purchased you a ticket to heaven. All the oil in Saudi Arabia is insufficient to buy you out of hell. All the Designer clothes you can accumulate could never make you acceptable to God. It took the blood of Jesus Christ to do that. ". . . you were not redeemed with perishable things like silver or gold . . . but with precious blood, as of a lamb unblemished and spotless, the blood of Christ" (1 Peter 1:18, 19).

When you sincerely want to know what you are worth, talk to your Designer. He only sees one label on you: JESUS!

Inside Out for
"Mirror, Mirror on the Wall . . ."

1. What qualities in your parents would you like to see reproduced in your children?

2. Think of someone who loves you. How does that person best demonstrate that love to you?

3. See John 15:13. How did Jesus demonstrate His love for you?

4. Describe some negative ideas or labels you may have received from your parents; other family members; your peers. How do these terms show up in your life-style?

5. Describe some positive input you have received from your parents and peers. How is this reflected in your life today?

6. If you were the new kid in class, how would your fellow students describe you after one month?

7. Are there some things that you are currently doing in order to be accepted? How can you tell the difference between doing what you want to do, and doing what is "acceptable"?

8. How does what you want to do compare with what your Designer wants you to do?

Against All Odds

7

Reggie and Laura are considered "the odd couple" on their Arizona State campus. Reggie is rich, handsome, and outgoing, while Laura is poor, plain, and shy. Reggie loves Laura, yet many of their fellow collegians cannot understand why.

Reggie explains it this way: "Laura is the only girl I've ever met who accepts me for who I am. She doesn't care that I come from a wealthy family. She loves *me*, not my money or my body. We've never had sex with each other. I'm glad I don't have to be a sexual superman in order to satisfy her. She is happy just being with me, and I feel lucky to have found someone who really cares."

What Reggie was saying has been borne out by a myriad of psychological studies. We all long to be loved and accepted for who we are. Though we don't want to be judged by our performance, we need to feel that we are able to succeed, and that we are competent to meet the needs of someone else. Dr. Maurice Wagner, a Christian counselor, expands these concepts in his valuable book, *The Sensation of Being Somebody* (Zondervan).

Dr. Wagner lists three basic emotional needs that are essential components of a healthy self-image:

1. A *sense of belonging*; to know that you are wanted, needed, accepted, and most of all, *loved*.
2. A *sense of worth and value*. This is that internalized, deep-down feeling that you have a purpose for being on this earth; to know you count, that your life is worth living, that you are accepted by others, and you are *acceptable* to yourself.
3. A *sense of being competent*. In this regard, competency is not merely saying, "Yes, I can do it." It is an entire outlook upon life that is optimistic rather than pessimistic; it is an attitude that says, "I can meet life head to head and enjoy doing it!"

These elements are as essential for a Christian as they are for a nonbeliever. Actually, these three components may make or break your Christian life! Let me explain:

I used to think that the three most important ingredients in a person's Christian life were *reading the Bible, praying,* and *going to church*. I still believe these disciplines are absolutely essential to a victorious Christian life. However, the more I counsel young adults, the more convinced I become that the most important factor in the progressive growth of a young Christian is a *positive, Christ-centered, biblically based self-image*. Without proper self-esteem—that sense of being loved, accepted, and competent—a person may perform the rituals of Christian living, but out of duty rather than devotion to the Designer.

Indirect Causes of Poor Self-Image

Why would any young adult *not* think highly of himself or herself? Why would you not feel that you belong, that you matter, that you can accomplish great things?

92

One cause of poor self-esteem is the fact that we live in a very negative world. Have you read the newspapers lately? Listened to the evening newscasts? It's a jungle out there! Add to that the threat of nuclear annihilation, and it's pretty easy to get depressed.

Still, a lot has to do with our attitude, doesn't it? Exciting, wonderful things happen every day, but you simply don't hear about them. Unfortunately, most of the positive events are not interesting headline material, as far as the news media are concerned.

Have you ever gone on vacation, and for a few days out of the year, totally ignored radio, TV, and the press? If you have never tried it, next vacation give it a chance. You'd be amazed how your outlook changes.

Certainly, we need to be knowledgeable about current events. As Christians, we cannot afford to live in isolation from the world around us. You can, however, limit or balance the amount of negative input you allow into your life.

Another indirect cause of low self-esteem is due to the fact that many modern-day young adults have been indoctrinated with Darwin's theory of evolution. If you discount the Genesis account of Creation and accept Mr. Darwin's nebulous theory that you evolved from a blob of goo, that in itself is self-deprecating. After all, if you are nothing more than a sophisticated ape, what difference does it make if you waste your life monkeying around?

I roared with laughter when I saw Clint Eastwood meet his match when he encountered his orangutan buddy, Clyde, in *Any Which Way But Loose*. Clyde is a brilliant beast, but I'd hate to think of him as my long-lost brother!

Yet, that is precisely the point of Darwinian evolution. No wonder so many teen-agers don't know who they are! If you don't know where you came from, you probably won't know why you are here or where you are going, and it will be impossible to become what you were created to be.

Aren't you glad that as Christians, we know that our heavenly Father lovingly designed us as His creations? You were not an accident of evolution. The Creator of the Universe intricately designed you as His crowning achievement.

Most of the causes of a poor self-image are internal rather than external. Your conscious mind collects and stores all the put-downs you receive and believe, the negative input you accept about yourself, the labels other people have put on you, the confusion between being a bad person and being a person who sometimes does something bad, the comparisons you make between yourself and other people, and of course, your past failures and sins.

Satanic Attacks on Your Self-Image

Satan can use any one or all of these weapons to bludgeon your self-image. Dr. David A. Seamands, whose ministry mightily influenced my thinking during my years at Asbury College and Asbury Theological Seminary, describes low self-esteem as "Satan's deadliest weapon." In his excellent work *Healing for Damaged Emotions* (Victor), Dr. Seamands discusses four ways the devil uses low self-esteem to defeat Christians:

First, he says that *low self-esteem paralyzes your potential*. Because of a poor self-image, many Christians, and especially many Christian young adults, waste their Designer-given gifts.

"I've just got to find myself," they rationalize their tragic condition. Unfortunately, they usually do find themselves ... about twenty years later, no closer to being what God wants them to be; they are simply twenty years older.

This kind of individual makes a great paper shuffler, mail opener, or office boy, but that's about it. They have great potential, but they are stalled in neutral; they're not going anywhere. They may get bumped a bit in either direction, but their overall progress will be negligible until they can overcome their personal inertia and reconstruct their self-image. In the meantime, they will continue to seek after that elusive butterfly of happiness, as they wait for their ship to come in—even though they never sent a ship out!

This kind of person is tied up in knots and tied down to a life far below his or her potential. It's as though their self-esteem has been paralyzed by Satan's stun-gun, and as a result, their power, potential, and possibilities slip out into oblivion.

Second, writes Dr. Seamands, *low self-esteem destroys your dreams.* Satan is a thief, and he would love to steal your dreams. No, I'm not talking about nightmares or daydreams. The devil would be *happy* to fill your head with those. I am referring, however, to the bold dreams that the Holy Spirit gives to us, the visions He wants us to have, and to see fulfilled.

One of the world's most successful soap salesmen is a fellow by the name of Dexter Yager of Charlotte, North Carolina. Actually, Dexter sold extensively more than soap in order to earn his fortune, working through the Amway Corporation. The product Dexter sells best is *Dexter!* With his positive self-image, Dexter Yager has become proficient at "selling himself" as a person. One of his favorite challenges to audiences who would aspire to walk in his footsteps is "Don't let anyone steal your dream!" In other words, be careful about associating with or adopting the attitudes of other people, who through their negative outlook and lack of self-esteem will rob you of the greatness that God has for you.

A classic illustration of this took place when the people of God, who had been delivered from the devil's bondage in Egypt, came to the borders of Canaan, God's dreamland for them (read: Numbers 13 and 14). God had promised His people a rich possession, a land flowing with milk and honey, a fantastic future. There was only one problem: the place that the Master Designer had created for His people was already inhabited.

Knowing that they might be in for a fight, Moses sent twelve spies into Canaan to check out the opposition. After six weeks, the scouts came back with their report.

"It's just like we heard!" they excitedly shared with the welcome party.

And all the people said, "Amen."

"It *is* a land flowing with milk and honey," the spies continued. "Look at these grapes. Look at these pomegranates! Why they're the biggest and best tasting we've ever seen. And, here. Taste some of this honey. Is that not something else?"

And all the people said, "Amen."

Then came the bad news. "*But*, there are giants in the land, and compared to them, we look like a bunch of grasshoppers."

And all the people said, "Oh, me, oh, my!"

"Therefore," concluded the spies, "we are not able to go in and take the land."

And all the people said, "We hear you, spies. Let's go back to Egypt!"

All the people except two (possibly four, if we count Moses and Aaron), Joshua and Caleb, two of the scouts, said, "Whoa! Not so. We are well able to possess the land, *because our God has given it to us!*"

Joshua and Caleb were not naive, optimistic, positive thinkers. Why, they had never even *heard* of Robert Schuller! They had the same facts as their fellow spies. They admitted the existence of the giants, the opposition, the obstacles, but the difference was in their attitude. *They believed God.* Their self-images were such that they refused to see themselves as grasshoppers ready to be stomped on. Instead, they saw themselves as God's men. Joshua and Caleb had the same data as the doubters; but they drew different conclusions, because they trusted their Designer, and they would not allow anyone else to steal their dreams.

Consequently, of over a million people who came out of Egypt, only *two*, Joshua and Caleb, eventually entered into God's Promised Land. The others were a reproach to their Designer's name. They dishonored Him, and as a result, spent the rest of their lives wandering around in circles throughout the wilderness, until they finally died. Due to their lack of self-esteem, they had allowed the devil to defeat and rob them of the Designer's dream for their future.

How is *your* dream? Is it still intact? If your dream has been damaged, delayed, or destroyed, it may be because the devil has deceived you into seeing yourself as a grasshopper. And we know that how we see ourselves is how we will perform. Don't let Satan steal your dream! Don't underestimate what your Designer wants to do in, through, and for you.

It's time that Christian young people begin to see Designer visions; that Christian older folk dream grand, Designer dreams (Joel 2:28; Acts 2:17).

Third, according to Dr. Seamands, *low self-esteem ruins your relationships*. Certainly, low self-esteem can ruin your relationship with your Creator. In many ways, if you willfully wallow in a low self-image, you are *insulting* the integrity of your Designer. After all, He made you. If you continue to devalue yourself by considering yourself as worthless or, at best, inferior even in an indirect way, you are saying, "God, You sure goofed when You made me. You did okay on some of my friends, and some of the famous people of this world, but You sure made a mess out of me."

Of course, it is only a small step from criticizing His *design* to criticizing and mistrusting the *Designer*. "You must not really love me, God. You don't truly care about me, do You? You're not the Person I thought You were. I guess the devil was right; You just want someone You can boss around. Well, it won't be *me!* See You later, God!" Chalk up one more victory for Satan because of your low self-esteem. Your resentment of yourself has caused you to resent the One who loves you most.

Similarly, a low self-image can destroy your relationships with other people. There seems to be a law in life: you don't always get what you want; you don't always get what you deserve; but you almost always get what you expect! If because of insecurity or inferiority complexes, you lack confidence in yourself, these shortcomings are projected onto your relationships with those closest to you. Many times, a low self-image tends to bring about the exact opposite of what you really want.

Mindy and Joel had been married for several years, but their relationship was a rocky one. Mindy's dad had run around on her mom when Mindy was a small child. Consequently, she grew up with her mother's words "Never trust a man! They're all alike!" echoing in her ears. Mindy brought her fears with her when she and Joel were married. Because of her own feelings of insecurity, Mindy was constantly mistrusting of her husband. Anytime another pretty girl said hello to Joel, Mindy got intensely jealous and accused him of flirting. "You're always making eyes at other girls!" she harangued him. "What's the matter? Don't I please you? Don't I make you happy?"

"Of course, you do," Joel would reassure her. "I can't help it if someone says hello to me!"

Still Mindy's suspicions persisted. Her apprehensions grew so absurd, Mindy would get angry if Joel watched an attractive woman on television. Finally, he couldn't take it anymore. Her false accusations alienated Joe to such an extent that he gradually withdrew his affections from Mindy, and eventually took them elsewhere. Mindy's low self-image had been the tool the devil used to turn her worst fears into reality, a self-fulfilled prophecy.

Low self-esteem can ruin your relationships with others in a variety of ways. Many individuals who suffer from poor self-concepts become downright obnoxious. They don't like themselves, and they make it difficult for anyone else to like them. They are hard to get along with, hard to work with, and especially hard to live with. They are critical and judgmental. Furthermore, since they don't like themselves, they often don't like and don't want to be with other people as well. They are self-conscious and oversensitive to others' opinions.

Jesus commanded us to "love thy neighbor as thyself," but without a proper self-esteem, it becomes impossible to have a proper value of anyone else.

Fourth on Dr. Seamand's list: *low self-esteem sabotages your Christian service.* Mother Teresa, the Nobel prize winner who works among the street people of Calcutta, has a pet saying: do "something beautiful for God." Yet, how many times have you missed out on opportunities to do just that, because of your low self-esteem?

"Oh, I could never sing in the choir. I can't carry a tune in a bucket."

"Be a part of an evangelistic visitation team? Why, I'd be scared to death. What if we were visiting in a home and somebody asked me to defend my faith? What would I do then?"

"What? *Me* teach a Sunday-school class? Ho, boy! You've got the wrong person. I'd ruin that class."

Do you hear it from others? Do you hear it coming out of your own mouth? Self-deprecation. You're telling God and yourself what you can't do, rather than what you can.

Now, obviously, not every one of us is gifted in every area. I have some friends that I prefer *not* to hear sing; at least, not unless they can be mixed back in the crowd . . . I mean, *way* back in the crowd. Not all of us are talented as teachers or witness leaders. But all of us can do "something beautiful for God."

Furthermore, since when did ability or talent become a prerequisite to service in Christ's Kingdom? All it takes is a dedication to Him, and a realization that He can use *your* life to touch others. Look at the people God has used down through history. Most of them were pretty unspectacular on their own—but they believed in God. And they believed in themselves, in that they were willing to allow Him to use what little bit they had.

I've always been enamored with the little boy who figured so prominently in "the feeding of the five thousand," as recorded in John 6. Read that account again and notice that everything Jesus used to perform this huge miracle was really quite small in itself. It was a *little* boy who brought five *little* loaves of bread, and two *little* fish to Jesus. The Middle Eastern bread is flat (almost like two pancakes stuck together), not at all like the large loaves to which we are accustomed. The fish were *opsarion*, small, sardinelike fish—not eighteen-inch rainbow trout like the ones you missed in the mountains!

Yet this *little* boy, with his *little* loaves and his *little* fish, had a *little* bit of *faith*. When he presented what little he had to Jesus, the Lord took it, blessed it, broke it, and was able to supernaturally minister to the needs of thousands that day. All because a little boy gave what little bit he had to the Master.

This is more than merely a cute Bible story: The little boy's actions and attitudes are what theologians refer to as *paradigmatic*, a pattern that our Designer gives to us and expects us to emulate. George Muller understood this.

As a young man, George wanted to do "something beautiful for God." He had a desire to help the street orphans in England. Though his desire was great, George's wallet was empty. He had only the equivalent of about fifty cents, and he felt that God wanted him to give away even that. Obediently, George gave the fifty cents. And God gave him back fifty cents more.

Right there, George Muller learned an invaluable lesson that many of us only talk about: "You can't outgive God." George continued to give to God and to pray for the Lord's provision. And God refused to let His man down. George Muller sent out no letters asking for money. In fact, he made a point of never revealing his need of financial assistance to any human being, but instead, depended upon God to supply what was required to do His work. Consequently, the Lord used George Muller to begin a ministry with just a few orphans in a rented house in Bristol, England, which soon blossomed into a huge complex of buildings, *housing more than two thousand children*. Before George turned the orphanages over to someone else, late in his life, God blessed him with more than two million dollars to use for His glory. And George used every penny of it to help more orphans.

Though George Muller was an eminently humble man, and

had a strong sense of his own sinfulness, he would not allow Satan to deceive him into believing that he was useless in the Designer's Kingdom. Instead, he threw himself upon the mercy of God, and then into the magnificent mission of God.

Don't allow Satan to sabotage your Christian service by sinking your self-esteem. Don't allow him to ruin your relationships, or destroy your dreams, or paralyze your potential. Rise up, and do something beautiful for God!

Inside Out for
"Against All Odds"

1. *In your life, what things do you do out of a sense of duty, a sense of devotion, a combination of both?*

2. *Describe some dreams you would like to see come true. How do you think these dreams fit with your Designer's plan for your life?*

3. *Can you think of a time when Satan robbed you through low self-esteem? How can you prevent the same thing from happening in the future?*

4. *Have you ever seen a relationship destroyed by low self-esteem? List three lessons that you learned from that situation.*

5. *Think back on opportunities to serve the Lord you may have missed in the past because of a poor self-image. How could you have taken advantage of those opportunities had your self-esteem been higher?*

6. *George Muller was a man of faith. What is there that you want to do that can only be completed through your Designer's supernatural assistance?*

A New Attitude

8

Lisa Welchel, the popular actress and singer who plays on television's "The Facts of Life," sums up the secret to her success: "Since I was ten years old, I knew that I would be loved no matter what. I don't have to perform and be a good person. If I blow it, I blow it. But the Lord still stands there with open arms to commend me. When you know you are totally accepted for who you are, then it's easier to say to others, 'Accept me if you want to. If you don't, it's okay. I'll just run home to Daddy' " (*Possibilities*, Sept./Oct. 1984).

Obviously Lisa has a positive self-image, but notice: it is not based upon what Hollywood says about her; neither is it centered in whether she is a success or not, nor what she looks like, nor how well she performs. Her security is based upon what her Designer says about her.

"The Lord has given us values that are really for our own benefit," says Lisa. "He's looking out for me. I try to keep in mind that it's for my own happiness. He knows better than I."

You Belong to the Designer

The first step toward overcoming low self-esteem is understanding that your Designer loves and accepts you unconditionally, no strings attached, just the way you are. You don't have to try to earn brownie points with God by doing good deeds, cleaning up your act, giving money to the church, or by becoming a religious person. Of course you don't deserve God's love, but neither can you destroy it. Nothing you do can deter God's love for you. Now don't misunderstand! Some of your actions may make Him angry; He may discipline you severely, but He will never cease to love you. Even if you choose to reject His love and decide to race into hell, He will continue to love you. On the positive side, if you belong to Him, you are part of His "Forever Family." God is not sitting in heaven saying, "Let's see, how can I kick him [or her] out of the Kingdom." No! He wants you in His family. Astounding as it may seem, the Creator of all things *wants you!*

The knowledge that your Designer loves and accepts you should make accepting yourself a lot easier. After all, wouldn't it be the height of arrogance for you to despise someone that God loves so unconditionally? Well, that *someone* is *you*. What right do you have to put down what the Designer has honored so highly, paid for so fully, planned and provided for so completely, and values so dearly?

Get it straight. God accepts you. You can accept yourself. If other people can accept you, great! If not, that's their problem, not yours. However, when you know that *you* are freely accepted by your heavenly Father, you can more readily accept other people for what they are.

A successful Christian songwriter and I were talking shop at a Nashville songwriter's symposium. He surprised me when he candidly revealed, "Bill and Gloria Gaither's composition 'I Am Loved' used to be my *least* favorite Christian song."

"Why?" I asked, the astonishment evident in my voice.

"Oh, you know," he answered sardonically. "All that talk about 'I am loved, you are loved.' When I first heard that song, I thought, 'Come on, Bill. Come on, Gloria. You can write better than that! What kind of syruppy, candy-coated, Christian schmaltz is that, anyhow?' "

"And now?" I queried.

"Well, now, it's one of my *favorite* songs," he replied with a smile.

"What happened? What made the difference?" I pressed him.

"You see, when I first came to this town, I had a pretty bad attitude. Toward other people, toward myself, and especially toward God. But then I became a Christian, and I realized that God loves me. I didn't have to compete for His love anymore. There was plenty to go around! That's when I became free enough to love other people. On the way, I found that I could accept myself, as well."

Not only is your Designer the One who loves you most; as that songwriter discovered, He is the One who loves you the most when you are at your worst! Despite your human frailties, He loves you and accepts you.

Forgive or Forget It

A second step toward overcoming a poor self-image is to get a grasp on God's forgiveness, purchased for us by Christ's death and His Resurrection. This, in turn, gives you a new sense of worthiness, value, and best of all, *acceptability* before God. You can stand before Him unashamed and confident, because you know you are clean. The Designer Himself has washed you. "He saved us, not on the basis of deeds which we have done in righteousness, but according to His mercy, by the washing of regeneration and renewing by the Holy Spirit, whom He poured out upon us richly through Jesus Christ our Savior" (Titus 3:5, 6).

Unquestionably, it's easy to feel worthless, especially when you've had so much unsolicited help at it. Maybe your parents' impossible expectations, or their otherwise poor job of parenting caused your self-esteem to plunge. Perhaps peer pressure and family rivalries contributed to your current negative feelings about yourself. Certainly, your own sins and failures are major factors in your self-image.

In any case, forgiveness is imperative. First, you must seek and receive the forgiveness of God. Second, you must forgive yourself and accept as truth the fact that you are forgiven. Then, you must extend forgiveness to those who have hurt you.

Here is where it gets sticky. All of us have been hurt by somebody, but if you allow that hurt to develop into bitterness, you will be wrapping a ball and chain around your self-esteem. Furthermore, Jesus made it clear on several occasions that unforgiveness on your part toward somebody else can destroy His whole offer of forgiveness to you! He said, "For if you forgive men for their transgressions, your heavenly Father will also forgive you. But if you do not forgive men, then your Father will not forgive your transgressions" (Matthew 6:14, 15).

When you hold onto unforgiveness, bitterness, hatred, and the desire for revenge, you have a very difficult time sensing God's presence in your life. It seems like He is not there, doesn't it? It's like He's moved a million miles away. You may read the Bible, but without His Presence, the Book seems filled with mere meaningless words. You pray, and your petition gets stuck on the ceiling, or perhaps bounces back at you.

You cry out, "Come on, God! What's going on here? Get with it!"

But He says something like, "No! You get *out* of it. Get your fist out of the pipe. Quit blocking the flow of my forgiveness."

One of the most impressive pictures I have ever seen was the one of Pope John Paul II visiting his would-be assassin, Ali Agca in prison. It would have been easy for the pope to write the boy off—to say "Good for him. That's what he deserves.

And worse!" But he didn't. He went to that man's jail cell, talked with him, prayed with him, and forgave him.

The pope realized something that we oftentimes forget or fail to understand: *Forgiveness must be initiated by us.* Most of us allow unforgiveness to fester, assuming that someday the person who offended us will return and apologize. That's wonderful when it happens, but many times it doesn't. Meanwhile, we continue to hold onto our grudge, thinking that we are hurting our offender, when all the while, that unforgiveness is like a cancer eating away at our relationship with Christ, and at our self-esteem. For God's sake, and for your own sake, let go of it before it destroys *you.*

Perhaps you have parents who inflicted horrible hurts upon you, physically, verbally, emotionally, or all three. Maybe it was long ago, or maybe it was last week. Regardless, Jesus says, "Forgive!"

Possibly you have brothers and sisters who always put you down, or let you down when you needed them the most. Maybe friends or other family members teased you, embarrassed you, made fun of you, or humiliated you. Jesus says, "You forgive them."

Maybe your best friend betrayed you, or your sweetheart rejected you, or your youth leader or pastor let you down. Whatever the case, you *must* let them off the hook. And do it *now.*

Delayed Response

Sometimes we say, "Well, okay, God. If I have to forgive them in order to keep from going to hell, I will. But can't I just hang on to my grudges a little longer? Can't I compromise just a bit? Can't I make that person pay for hurting me? Can't I make him suffer? Won't You allow me to hurt her the way she hurt me? Can't we hold this thing over his head and watch him fry? God, I sure enjoy watching that person sweat and squirm! Oooh! It feels so good! Can't I just withhold that forgiveness a short while longer?"

And the King of all Creation gets up off His heavenly throne and declares, "*No!* Not if you expect Me to cancel *your* debt! (*See* Matthew 18:23–35). If you expect to be forgiven, then you must be a *forgiver.*"

I'm not asking you to *feel* forgiving. I'm not asking you to condone what that person did, or even to understand. Forgiveness is much more than a mushy, gushy feeling. Forgiveness is a *choice.* It is an act of your will, in which you say, "I choose to forgive my mother." Or "I choose to forgive my former boyfriend or girlfriend"; "I am making a conscious decision of my will to forgive that person who hurt me."

A strong possibility exists that the party you forgive may never find out about your personal deliverance from the bondage of the past. Maybe that person has moved away from town, or died, or has gotten married and is not in contact with you any longer. That's okay. The resentment and bitterness has been thwarting *your* self-esteem and *your* relationship with your Designer. If ever an opportunity arises in which you can comfortably confront your offender, pray much about that possibility, and then follow the Holy Spirit's leading precisely. Many times, however, the extension of forgiveness which so significantly impacts upon your self-image does not even have to be spoken directly to the offender in order to take effect. It can be between God and you, with perhaps the addition of a trusted friend or counselor.

When you honestly forgive those who hurt you, the battle against low self-esteem will dramatically turn in your direction. Try it and see if your self-image and your sense of worthiness does not immediately begin to rise.

A Friend in Need

I once saw a bumper sticker that read: A FRIEND IN NEED . . . IS A PEST!

That's what the world will tell you, and that's what a lot of Christians who are struggling with their own self-image problems will tell you, too. Nevertheless, if you can find one faithful friend in whom you have confidence, and with whom you can share your own inferiority feelings and insecurities, you will be taking a major step up the ladder of self-esteem. There is something redemptive and liberating about confessing our sins, our faults, and our failures, one to another. The Bible says, "Therefore, confess your sins to one another, and pray for one another, so that you may be healed. The effective prayer of a righteous man can accomplish much" (James 5:16).

Be extremely cautious in your selection of such a friend. Choose one who is honest and trustworthy, someone with whom you can share your deepest thoughts and feelings without fear that they will be broadcast all over town next week. Seek out someone whose opinions and advice you respect, someone who can sensitively evaluate and feed back to you what you tell them. Don't share these intimacies with someone who, you know, will simply reinforce your own inferiorities. Look for someone whose suggestions you will follow if redirection is necessary.

Talk to that person often, and on a prolonged basis. Don't expect results overnight. Your self-image wasn't formed in a day, and it won't be reconstructed overnight either. This is going to be a process, and your friend will need to be there a week, a month, maybe a year down the road, so choose carefully.

Ask your friend to honestly tell you whether he or she thinks your feelings are justified; do you have areas where your self-image is distorted? Then begin to explore ways of changing your self-image. Read this book and discuss it together, as well as other books dealing with self-esteem. (See Suggested Reading List.)

If you don't have a friend who can help you in this capacity, perhaps a local pastor will be able to meet with you over a period of time and act as your sounding board. Pastors are extremely busy, though, and finding one who can give you the kind of time you will need is not as easy as it seems.

If not a pastor, possibly a professional counselor can help you. The entire field of Christian psychology is expanding, and competent counselors are available nowadays. Don't feel like a weirdo for seeking help. In fact, you will be just the opposite. You will be wiser and more able to pull out of the depression caused by a poor self-image.

Certainly, your friend or counselor should be an encouragement to you, not a drag on your spiritual strength or your opinion of yourself. Remember, you caught your self-image like you catch a cold, from someone close to you. Nothing will help redirect that self-image as much as positive, honest encouragement from someone close to you whose opinions you respect. We all need encouragement; you are no exception.

Practical Friendship

Of course your friend can greatly assist you in the practical areas of improving your self-image. He or she can encourage you to read biographies and autobiographies of people who have had a significant impact upon the world. Read the stories of Abraham Lincoln, Thomas Edison, Billy Graham, Pat Robertson, and others. Read about the people who have done what you would like to be doing and learn from them. If they are still living, listen to them speak, either in person, on tape, or on television. Observe and absorb their performances.

Your friend can also encourage you to smile. Give that person permission to gently remind you concerning your facial features. You will feel better about yourself when you are smiling, and the people with whom you come in contact will feel better about you.

Along these same lines, your friend can encourage you to dress up your appearance. As Christians, we should never be so foolish as to judge another person by his or her outward appearance. Nevertheless, neither should we be so foolish as to think that *our* appearance does not make a statement to the world. Your outward appearance is a reflection of how you feel and how you regard yourself on the inside. If other factors are equal, the person who looks sharp will get the job, or be selected. Certainly your self-image should never be dependent upon your looks, but you can use your appearance to positively bolster your self-image. Zig Ziglar, one of the most self-confident fellows I've ever heard, admitted, "My own image improved when I lost thirty-seven pounds" (*See You at the Top*, Pelican).

Get your friend to help you develop a list of your best qualities, write them down, and then refer to them often. Ask your friend to tell you what he or she honestly likes about you and mark those items in your PLUS column. Find out your weaknesses, too, and list them as areas that you plan to improve.

Your friend can also help you to avoid negative input that would sabotage your efforts to improve your self-image. Unquestionably, your picture of yourself will be influenced positively or negatively through the material you allow to enter your mental computer. Steer clear of books, movies, television programs, music or other input that you know are going to bring you down. Your friend can be a big help here. Go places together. Read the same books. Watch the same movies. Keep your mental input on the positive side.

Obviously, a good friend can be a tremendous help in rebuilding your self-image. Don't give up trying to find such a person, but on the other hand, don't let a lack of comradeship keep you from developing your own plan of action. Eleanor Roosevelt battled for years with a negative self-concept. She kept at it, though, and slowly began to see herself differently. Eventually, she became one of the best-loved and most powerful women in America, and not simply on her husband's coattails. It is she who is credited with saying, "Nobody can make you feel inferior without your permission."

Down With the Dirty Old Man!

A dirty old man is trying to destroy your attempts at renovating your self-image. Paul implies that this dirty old man is your sinful nature, the old you, who was totally enslaved by sin. The Apostle instructs you to "... lay aside the old self, which is being corrupted in accordance with the lusts of deceit, and that you be renewed in the spirit of your mind, and put on the new self, which in the likeness of God has been created in righteousness and holiness of the truth" (Ephesians 4:22–24).

Paul is basically saying, "Don't let the devil deceive you any longer! Don't accept his false impressions of who you are. Lay those things aside, and take your picture of yourself from your Designer. Allow His Holy Spirit to reprogram your computer so you can see yourself the way He sees you."

It is the Holy Spirit who is the great Enabler; He provides the power to live the Christian life the way God intended it to be lived, under His power, not simply in reliance upon our own human resources.

I was staying at a summer house on gorgeous Lake Lanier, near Gainesville, Georgia, when I realized this truth more fully. Each afternoon, I would slip down to the docks and watch the boats skimming across the water in the glistening Georgia sunshine. I noticed the sailboats were driven about by every change in the wind currents, but the motorboats had their power on board with them.

I thought, *That's the difference between depending on our own resources and depending upon the Holy Spirit for power. God wants us to have power on board, power within, so we won't be blown around by every wind of doctrine, or every blowhard who says something negative about us.* I recalled one of my favorite verses of Scripture, "But you shall receive power when the Holy Spirit has come upon you ..." (Acts 1:8). He wants to give us that power, that *dunamis,* dynamite type power within us to live victoriously.

Results of a Renewed Self-Image

As you cooperate with the Holy Spirit in the reprogramming of your self-image, not only will you have a new power, you will sense a new purity, a new (or renewed) purpose in life, and a peace in your heart and mind unlike anything the world has to offer (*See* John 14:27). These results are directly related to having the Holy Spirit's Presence on board, *within* you!

When you entrust your self-image to the Holy Spirit, you can expect the Bible to become a different Book to you. The same Spirit who *inspired* the Word of God will *illumine* the Scriptures in your mind. Furthermore, prayer will take on a new dimension for you. It will cease to be simply a "Christmas list" with an *Amen* on the end of it. Your prayer time will become genuine communication with your Creator! In addition, as you see the Spirit of Christ working in and through your personality, you will sense a new capacity and desire to praise the Lord Jesus, to worship Him, and to bear witness of what He has done in your life. Your life itself will become a testimony of His greatness.

Perhaps some of the most dramatic results of His renewing your heart and mind will take place in the personal, practical, nitty-gritty areas of your life. For one thing, *you won't have to have your own way any longer*. Your self-image will be secure enough that you can give up what you want in order to do what your Designer wants. Jesus summed up this remarkable attitude in His prayer in the Garden of Gethsemane, when He said, "Father, if Thou art willing, remove this cup from Me; yet not My will, but Thine be done" (Luke 22:42).

A second practical result of the Holy Spirit's reprogramming of your self-image will be: *you won't have to look good anymore!* No longer will you be oppressed by the nagging need to impress everyone with how great *you* are. The attention will be directed toward your Designer. "For from Him and through Him and to Him are all things. To Him be the glory forever" (Romans 11:36).

Paradoxically, as the Holy Spirit renovates your self-image, you will become increasingly more comfortable with yourself. You will be able to honestly say, "I like me!" without being boastful or proud. You won't have to flaunt who you are or what you have accomplished in life, or who you know, or what possessions you own. You will have an accurate picture of who you are in Christ. You can confidently proclaim, "I like what Jesus is doing in me!"

A third result of the Spirit's restoration will be: *you won't have to defend yourself anymore*. More specifically, you won't have to defend your *self*. Your self-image will not be dependent upon what others think, say, or do about you. Therefore, you will be free from having to have the last word.

The early disciples discovered how liberating this could be when, after they were filled with the Holy Spirit, they were able to confidently stand before the same men who had condemned Jesus to the cross and proclaim, ". . . Whether it is right in the sight of God . . . you be the judge; for we cannot stop speaking what we have seen and heard" (Acts 4:19, 20). These disciples didn't have to fight or argue anymore. They knew *who* they were, and they knew *whose* they were.

Finally, as you allow the Holy Spirit to reconstruct your self-image, you will be pleasantly surprised to discover that *you don't need to please "the crowd" any longer*. You are free! Jesus said, "You shall know the truth, and the truth shall make you free" (John 8:32). When you know the truth about who you are, you won't get swept along by the currents of peer pressure or public opinion. You can dare to be different. Your values will be different. Your goals will be different. Your actions and responses will not be determined by what a sinful world says, but by what your loving Designer desires. It may not be the easy way to walk, but I guarantee you, it will be worth it, now and forever!

One of the most profound influences upon my life has been the writings of Samuel Logan Brengle. Brengle gave up an opportunity to pastor one of the largest churches in Mid-America in order to join the ranks of the Salvation Army, when that organization was just getting established in the United States. One of his early assignments was in Danbury, Connecticut, where Brengle's entire congregation often numbered less than a dozen people.

Determined to reach Danbury with the Gospel, each evening Brengle marched up and down its streets singing, preaching, and praising God.

One night, while marching with only two of his parishioners at his side, a large, lame black and a little hunchback girl, Brengle and his "congregation" were bravely singing a song, ironically entitled, "We're the Army That Shall Conquer." Suddenly, the small group came abreast a large and imposing Methodist Church. Let Brengle's biographer, Clarence W. Hall, describe the inner conflict that ensued in *Samuel Logan Brengle: Portrait of a Prophet:*

> His glance swept across the broad front and traveled upward to the tall spire; the great church seemed to look down upon him and his little flock with infinite condescension and derision. And immediately a mocking voice broke out across the song to smite him in the heart: "You fool, you! You might have been the pastor of a great church like that. But here you are instead, the pastor of a big Negro and a little hunchback!" For a moment his voice faltered in the ambitious assertion concerning his "conquering" Army, and he was inclined to agree with his tempter. Only for a moment, however. In the next he had remembered all God's dealings with him, and, turning his eyes back to his pitifully small group, smiled to them with encouragement and pride, swung his arm vigorously and was leading them again in "We're the Army That Shall Conquer!"

Samuel Logan Brengle didn't need the acclaim of the world to reinforce his self-image. He didn't have to look good, defend himself, or have the last word. He knew that he didn't have to please anyone but Jesus. When you know that, *nothing else matters!*

Self-Image and the Unselfish Christian

For the Christian, developing a positive self-image is not the end of the road. You must never allow your self-image to become stagnant or stale. Keep your heart and mind sensitive to new and better ways of improving your self-esteem. The improving of your self-image is not like taking a course in school and then saying, "Now, I've got it. I have passed Self-Image 101." Neither is it a cure for all our spiritual problems. It is a step—a major step to be sure—but just a step, toward becoming more effective in our daily Christian lives. A Christian should seek to improve his or her self-esteem because in doing so, he or she will actually be *less* self-centered, and more Christ-oriented and others-oriented. Perhaps, had Adam and Eve never sinned, all this talk about self-image may have been superfluous. Nevertheless, we will not be judged by their relationship with the Lord but our own.

In the heart of every true believer burns a desire to be pleasing in God's sight and effective in His service. That's why your self-image is so important to your overall functioning within the body of Christ. Undoubtedly, the two factors that will most largely influence your relationship with other people are: (1) your concept of the Designer; and (2) your concept of yourself. It is next to impossible to be a genuine servant of Jesus without a healthy self-esteem. Only those who have an accurate handle on their own self-worth will be able to take up the towel and washbasin and be a servant to others. Without a proper self-image, you *may* pour yourself out in service to others, but it will be out of fear, intimidation, self-righteousness, or another improper motive. You will feel threatened every time someone else seems to get ahead of you, or looks better than you do in the eyes of others. The temptation to make yourself look better by putting someone else down will always be there until you begin to cooperate with the Holy Spirit in the renovation of your self-image.

With a healthy self-esteem, you will be able to treat every person as a valuable, special creation of God. You won't be intimidated when you encounter someone better-looking than you, or more talented, or with a higher IQ, or more important, or someone who possesses more (or less) of any other human trait. You will be free to love and accept that person, because you know that you, too, have been given Designer Genes!

Okay. Now that you have begun to improve your self-image, what do you do with all this newfound self-awareness? Let me show you how you can take this key and use it to help you unlock the door to all that your Designer wants you to be. First, complete Inside Out for this chapter.

Inside Out for
"A New Attitude"

1. *How does the knowledge that you belong to your Designer affect your daily life?*

2. *When other people don't accept you, how do you usually respond? Compare your response with Lisa Welchel's.*

3. *Give a description of an instance when, if you were God, you would have turned your back on somebody like you. Why do you suppose He didn't?*

4. *Peter asked Jesus, ". . . how often shall my brother sin against me and I forgive him? . . ." Read Jesus' answer in Matthew 18:21–35. What did Jesus mean?*

5. *Think of somebody who has hurt you somewhere in your past. Write that person's name on a piece of paper and a brief description of the pain he or she inflicted upon you. As an act of your will, say, "I forgive _____ ." Now, as a tangible indication that the grudge is gone, tear the paper into as many pieces as possible, and throw it away. Give thanks to God that He has released you from the past!*

6. *Describe the characteristics of a true friend. How can you be that kind of friend?*

7. *Attempt to read at least one book or watch one television program this week concerning the life of a person who has made a positive impact upon our world.*

8. *Is there a special friend to whom you look for guidance and encouragement? What characteristics about that person's life would you like to adopt in your own? (See Proverbs 13:20.)*

9. *What are you doing in your life right now that you could not possibly do without the power of the Holy Spirit?*

10. *Is there an area in which you have compromised your Christian life? If so, in a specific way, how can you get victory over that area by cooperating with the Holy Spirit?*

11. *Why is having a good self-image necessary in effective Christian service?*

12. *Find three older friends who have been Christians longer than you have been. Ask them to share their worst failures and their grandest victories with you. What have you learned from their experiences that will help you in your own life?*

What You See Is What You Get!

Bob Moawad, a popular campus lecturer, tells a bizarre but true story about a man who somehow got himself locked into a railroad refrigerator car. With the door shut tightly, and no apparent escape, he sat down to await the inevitable death by freezing or suffocation, whichever came first.

To pass the time, he decided to chronicle his demise by writing his thoughts on the wall of the railroad car. His first statement was: "It's getting colder in here." Later he wrote, "I'm freezing to death!" A few hours later he scribbled, "Nothing to do. Nothing to do but wait. . . ." Several hours later, he wrote, "These may be my last words . . ." and they were. He died.

When the door was finally opened, the rescuers found him dead, but the temperature of the car was fifty-six degrees! The refrigeration unit on the car had been out of order for some time and was not functioning at the time of the man's death.

He died, apparently, because he saw himself as doomed with no way out.

For that man, as for all of us, the thing he feared or expected to happen came to pass. The old adage, "Life is a self-fulfilling prophecy" held true for him. It will usually be true in your life as well. Remember: how you "see" yourself will determine how you will perform and what you can expect to receive in life.

Drawing upon the improvements you have been making in your self-image, it is possible, then, to "see" yourself performing at increasingly higher levels in every area of life. Psychologists refer to this as the process of *visualization*. Don't let that term throw you. Basically, it means to see yourself now as the person you want to become in the future, doing what you want to be doing, and being the type of person your Designer and you want you to be.

Diff'rent Strokes

I owe my golf game to Denis Waitley, in whose outstanding book *Seeds of Greatness* I first discovered the technique of visualization.

For years, prior to reading Waitley's book, I "saw" myself as a nongolfer. Not because the game didn't interest me, but because I had tried playing golf on a few occasions. I was awful! But at least, I was consistent. I invariably scored in the low nineties—for the first nine holes! I was so bad that in one tournament, I was given an award—for being the absolute *worst* golfer on the course. I think the club management figured that if they humiliated me badly enough, I wouldn't return to their course. But like a glutton for punishment, I kept going back. I do hold some dubious distinctions from those days, though. For example, who else do you know who could hit a golf ball down the fairway and actually *lose* yardage? (I don't know why they ever put that rock in the middle of the fairway, anyhow.)

Finally, in anger and frustration, I gave up. I said, "It's a silly game. You have the ball in your hand, and then you knock it away, and then have to go and chase it. What's the point?"

When any of my friends or family would invite me to play golf with them (kind souls), I conveniently had something more important to do.

"We've got tee-times for Tuesday at two o'clock, Ken. Do you want to go along?"

"Tuesday, eh? Two in the afternoon? Nope. Tuesday afternoon is usually the time when I pair my socks."

For the next twelve years, I never touched a golf club. Still, deep inside, I longed to be able to line the ball up on the first tee, and drive it a few hundred yards down the fairway, rather than dribble it off toward the ladies' tee, as I had done in the past.

While lying on the beautiful pink sand of Bermuda's Coral Beach, I began to read Denis Waitley's *Seeds of Greatness*. In it, he outlined the way to go about visualizing successful performances in your mind. I read with keen interest as Dr. Waitley described prisoners of war, who had practiced golf in their minds while in captivity, and then upon their return home found that they had retained or improved their golfing abilities without actually lifting a club! The ultimate test of the validity of Denis Waitley's theories, I figured, would be *my* golf game. If visualization could work on my game, it would work on anything! I didn't have the courage to experiment on the coastlined links in Bermuda, where the water traps are the Atlantic Ocean, but as soon as I returned to my home in Pennsylvania, I called for tee-times.

Out on the course, all of my old fears and memories of failure came flooding over me like the Bermuda tradewinds.

"Are you sure you want to subject yourself to this?" my brother John joked, as we prepared to tee off.

"I've got nowhere to go but up!" I responded. I stepped up to the ball and prepared to swing. Just before I brought the club up over my shoulders, I mentally rehearsed the proper way to swing, and where I wanted the ball to go.

"Straight out the fairway, right up there by the big tree," I thought out loud. As I brought the club back, I hung suspended in time for a moment, visualizing the sight, sound, and feel of a beautiful drive out the center of the fairway. I saw myself swinging through and meeting the ball solidly with the drive. Finally, I whipped the club through my swing.

"Crack!" the sound of the club meeting the ball resounded through the trees as the white sphere shot off the tee like a bullet. It soared through the blue sky, racing past the area where my drives usually dribbled off the fairway, and kept on going. Going! Going! Right up near the big tree, exactly where I wanted to be!

"Yahooo!" I shouted, forgetting all of my golf etiquette for the moment. "I did it! I did it! I can do it! Denis Waitley, you're a genius."

Several golfers stared at me rather strangely as I jubilantly started toward my ball. I didn't care. I had visualized a good shot, and it had worked.

Before you think that I turned pro overnight, let me tell you that I am still a long way from losing my amateur status. I have, however, taken a few golf lessons from a professional teacher, and continued to incorporate his advice into my visualizations. As such, my score has improved significantly. I'm still golfing in the low nineties—only now, that score is for eighteen holes rather than nine! With the help of a few more lessons, I am planning to visualize my way into the low eighties next season, or maybe break into the seventies.

Visualization is really nothing new. Great performers in every field have been aware of this secret for years. Athletes, astronauts, public speakers, airplane pilots, and a variety of other professionals have long recognized the value of mental simulation and rehearsal. Recent research at Stanford University has substantiated that your subconscious mind cannot tell the difference between a real experience and a mental experience, one that is vividly imagined in your mind. In fact, it may well be that your subconscious experiences are more influential in controlling your performance than are your conscious experiences. This can work for you or against you.

For example, you know that you have a big test coming up in Mr. DeFazio's class, so you really hit the books in preparation for it. Yet, you keep saying, "Oh, boy! This is going to be a rough test. I just know I'm going to blow it. No matter how much I study, I can never do well on one of DeFazio's tests. Where does he get those questions?"

You spend all night in study and preparation, and the moment you walk into Mr. DeFazio's classroom, your mind goes blank. As he passes out the test papers, you smell the mimeograph fluid on the paper, and it acts like an anesthetic. A giant eraser seems to wipe clean any knowledge you ever had concerning DeFazio's material. Fifteen minutes after the exam, you can remember the material exactly as you studied it. What happened?

Basically, you visualized yourself failing. You programmed your mental computer in advance and "saw" yourself flunking the exam. Your subconscious mind, not knowing whether this was factual information or not, accepted it as truth because it was something you had vividly imagined. Therefore, your subconscious mind helped you to fulfill your own prophecy.

You Have to See Straight

Here is where your self-image really comes into play. Your self-image acts as a "comfort zone," that area in which you comfortably see yourself performing. For this reason, it is almost impossible to *consistently* perform on a level higher than you see yourself. Your self-image acts similar to a thermostat in your home. If the temperature falls below the current setting, the thermostat will kick on the heat. If the temperature rises above the current setting, the thermostat will kick off the heat, or perhaps turn on the air conditioning, in order to bring the temperature back into the comfort zone.

Similarly, your self-image will pull you back into your comfort zone when it comes to your performance. If you perform better than you see yourself, your self-image will bring you down; if you perform worse than you see yourself, your self-image will pull you up.

For instance, if you have labeled yourself as a poor gymnast, you are probably going to remain a poor gymnast. If you say, "I can never do a cartwheel right," you never will! If you say, "I always fall off the parallel bars," try as you might, you will be unable to stay on those skinny wooden rails.

Some students say things like, "I always get Cs. No matter how much I study, I am a C student. I know it, my teachers know it, my parents know it, and so does everyone else. I'm a two-point-grade average and always will be."

This kind of self-image will perpetuate itself. If you see yourself as an average student, even if you start off a semester with straight As, you will somehow or other blow enough tests, miss enough classes, insult enough teachers, or whatever it takes, to get back into your comfort zone, your "C-level." When you get a paper with an A on it, your self-image responds, "That's not like you! You were just lucky." It will pull you back into the zone in which you see yourself. Likewise, if you fall below your usual two-point average, your self-image will say, "That's not like you! You're not a D student; you're a C student."

Beat the System

The secret to beating this system is visualization. Here's how it works. Think of your mind as a computer, and your self-image as a video cassette recorder. Together, these two "machines" govern your actions. *You* program the computer, and *you* decide what images will be stored in your mental VCR. To raise your level of performance, you must first "record" the picture on your self-image video cassette. You can do this by mentally seeing yourself doing the activity you wish to do. This visualization must be vividly imagined and *in the first person.*

In other words, you must see the experience through *your own* eyes; it will do you little good to simply view yourself as a spectator would. You must sense the experience from your own inner perspective.

For example, if you have been having problems driving that beautiful, new *big!* family car, you must see yourself behind the wheel, expertly gliding in and out of traffic. Inhale that luscious "new-car smell." Feel the wheel in your hands; see the road through your own eyes; hear the traffic zooming by you in both directions. Blow the horn. Put on your turn signals. Feel the surge of power as you press down on the gas pedal. Smell the scent of flowers and feel the fresh air rushing against your face as you motor out into the country. Do all of this *in your mind*, as if you are actually driving the car.

Whatever else you do, don't visualize yourself playing bumper cars in the streets. Don't feel yourself shaking in your shoes as you slip in behind the wheel. You don't want to hear sounds of screeching tires, scraping metal, or tinkling glass. Don't smell the pungent odor of a radiator overheating. Don't even think about backing out of the driveway right into your neighbor's new car. Don't let yourself hear that awful thumping sound that comes when you open your car door into the car next to you in the mall parking lot. Don't allow your mind to entertain thoughts of your sparkling new car careening around a curve and tumbling over a cliff, as you see on television or in the movies.

Decide which picture you want to see. Then use your self-image and your mental computer to visualize yourself succeeding at what you want to do. *Concentrate on doing things right.* Don't dwell on the possible obstacles or opportunities for failure. Certainly you need to prepare and practice, using proper techniques and information. If you visualize yourself doing something the wrong way, you will be reinforcing your bad habits. When done correctly and repeatedly, though, your mental computer will retrieve the image from your mental VCR, and then translate that image into physical actions.

What You See Is What You Get!

To be effective, visualization takes *practice*, both mentally and physically. The old saying "Practice makes perfect" is not entirely true. *Perfect* practice makes perfect! But that's part of the beauty of visualization; in your mental practice, at least, you never have to fail. You can do it right every time, assuming you are working with correct information. Sooner or later, though, your mental practice must take to the field.

Gary Anderson, the handsome, young field-goal kicker for the Pittsburgh Steelers, is consistently among the top scoring players in the National Football League. He is a study in concentration, as twenty-one giants attempt to either protect Gary, or smear him before he can kick the football. Often he is called upon to perform in crucial, win-or-lose situations. Again and again, under intense pressure, with thousands of screaming fans looking on, and millions more watching on television, with human bodies crashing into each other all around him, Gary calmly boots the ball between the uprights.

How does he do it? "I just make sure my foot hits the ball!" quips Gary.

Actually, it is much more involved than that. It also requires practice, and lots of it. I've watched Gary Anderson in Steeler training camp, where he works for hours on end, kicking field goals until his entire body throbs from the impact of his foot blasting into the ball. Gary practices and prepares, knowing that when his opportunity in the limelight comes, he must be ready on a moment's notice.

As Gary jogs onto the field, his mind must be riveted on only one thing: kicking that football. "I can't worry about the pressure," says Gary, "or the noise of the crowd, or what the score is. I have to concentrate on the ball. Before I kick, all I see is the ball going through the goalposts."

To be effective, visualization must be *personal*; it must be *practiced*, and it also must be *positive*. In other words, visualize what you *want*, not what you don't want.

Golf Course Psychology

Come back to the golf course with me. Most courses have several water hazards you must hit the ball over or around. The course where I play most often has *eight* lakes or ponds that must be eluded. Several of the water hazards are directly in front of the tee areas.

Before I learned the secret of visualization, these ponds sucked up my golf balls faster than I could buy them. At times I thought sure I saw the ponds stretch, just to catch my shots.

Of course, the problem was not in the pond, the problem was in my mind. I'd come off the green, feeling good about the putt I had just put in the hole, and there, staring me in the face, was my worst fear.

"Oh, no! A water hole. I hate teeing off over water! I certainly don't want to hit this beautiful ball into the lake," I lamented, as I fondled my brand-new, orange Spalding Top Flite. "These things cost too much money, just to knock them into the pond."

So what would I do? I'd go back to my golf bag and dig out the oldest, dirtiest, cheapest, and most cut-up golf ball I could find.

"I'm not taking any chances of losing a good ball to this water," I announced to my playing partners. "I'm going to hit my *water ball!*"

Do you believe in predestination? I do. I know that some golf balls are predestined to spend their lives on the bottom of ponds—specially those balls that I designated as *water balls!*

"Whoosh!" went my golf club.

"Sploosh!" went my water ball, right where I had imagined it would go. I tipped my hat in a brief commemorative ceremony. I had buried another one.

What Do You Want?

You cannot visualize what you do not want. You *must* visualize what you want. For some reason, your mental computer and video tape player cannot understand a negative command. When you say, "*Don't* hit the ball into the water," your subconscious only receives the message, "Hit the ball into the water." If you want to avoid the water hazard, you need to visualize something like this: "I want to loft this shot right out there on the fairway, about seventy-five yards in front of the green."

Most professional musicians have learned this lesson. Rather than worrying about the mistakes they might make, they practice their music in their imaginations the way they want to perform it. Before I learned about visualization, I used to hatch a batch of butterflies in my stomach before every major ABRAHAM concert. I believed in Murphy's Law: "Anything that can go wrong will go wrong!"

One night, just before we went on stage, we decided to open the program with a new song, one that my brother and I had completed writing only a few minutes earlier. I was panic-stricken as I shared my fears with the other group members. "What if I can't remember how it goes?" I fretted. "I know I'm going to mess it up; you guys might be able to remember your parts, but I know I won't be able to remember mine. I just can't recall all the changes in the song without practicing it."

To make matters even worse, "PM Magazine," the nationally syndicated television program, was covering the concert in order to do a special report on contemporary Christian music.

"Come on, you guys," I wailed, "let's open up with another song. I'll never remember that one!"

"Oh, take it easy, Ken," the other group members tried to encourage me, "you'll do just fine."

"No, I won't. I know I won't!"

And I didn't. From the moment the stage lights came up, I was lost. I saw the television cameras, the crowd of people, the bright lights, and suddenly, I was in "la-la-land." I couldn't remember how the song started, what I was supposed to play in the middle, where the musical syncopations were to occur, or how to end the thing! I had allowed my fears to program my mental computer to forget the song, and my "negative confessions" were actualized to the note. Fortunately, the song was an up-tempo number, and the audience quickly caught the beat—which is more than I did—and they started clapping along to the music. Their exuberance was contagious, and I was able to finish the number on raw enthusiasm alone. The crowd went wild, clapping and cheering, whistling, and stomping their feet.

Afterward, one of the reporters covering the concert caught me backstage. "Hey, Ken. What was the name of that song you guys came on with tonight?"

"Oh, the first song? Oh, well, ah, you know, we just wrote that one for tonight, and we haven't even given it a title yet. It's just a new song we worked out this afternoon . . ."

"Oh! That's great! 'New Song.' That's a super title and a super song. Yessir, I like that 'New Song'!" He bustled by me to catch up with his cameraman.

I shook my head in wonder and said, "Thanks, Lord. You still perform miracles!"

The Team With Super Genes

You can find the process of visualization working every day in high schools and colleges. Has it ever occurred to you that some schools always seem to come out on top in sports? Other schools consistently sweep the academic scholarships. Another school is noted for its many merit awards for outstanding community services. Why is that? Do they simply have a better recruiting program? Do they have better teachers or coaches? Do they have a monopoly on a certain set of genes or chromosomes that breed successful students?

No! They have learned the secret of visualization. They dwell on what they *want,* not on what they *don't want.*

Joe Paterno and his Penn State Nittany Lions are a curious enigma to college football observers. In their dull, drab uniforms and black football cleats (some of the Penn State players still wear the high-top shoes that have been out of vogue since the late sixties), Paterno's players look like a newsreel from 1958. The university itself is located in the sleepy little town of State College, a lovely place to vacation when you want to "get away from it all," but hardly the kind of surroundings that would lure city slickers to the sidelines. Nevertheless, despite their rather nondescript appearance and unexciting location, Penn State football teams are consistently among the best in the nation. Paterno has taken his Penn State players to postseason bowl games in seventeen of the past twenty years.

How do they do it? How does Paterno keep cranking out winners in an atmosphere that would seemingly perpetuate mediocrity?

It's because Paterno's Penn Staters see themselves as winners. They dwell on what they want, another national championship, not another losing season. Paterno teaches his players that life is more than football games; they are only in competition with themselves. If they do the best they can and still lose, Paterno teaches them that they are winners. If they win a ball game, but don't perform up to their potential, Paterno considers that a loss.

Coach Paterno also instills within his players the habit of dwelling upon what went *right* in the last game, or the past season, rather than what his players did wrong. Certainly, game films are scrutinized meticulously to discover why errors occurred, but once the mistake has been noted and corrected, then the emphasis is placed upon reinforcing the kind of play that Penn State has come to expect.

If you think about it, that's what our heavenly Coach does too! Yes, He convicts us of sin, righteousness, and judgment (John 16:8); He shows us our errors, our failures, our willful rebellion, and our sin. But, then, He gives us opportunity to repent and to make right our mistakes, insofar as possible. Once that has been done, He fully forgives and never brings the matter up again. He doesn't say, "Son, remember that sin that you repented of three years ago? I want to talk to you about that again." Instead, He washes that sin away, and gives us a clean slate. He will keep what was good and right about our lives, and place the emphasis there.

Furthermore, He wants us to get so wrapped up in a loving relationship with Him, that we shift our attention away from simply avoiding sin and begin to concentrate on doing right, living holy Christian lives. Rather than continuing to beat ourselves for sins of the past, we need to learn how to dwell on successful Christian living in the present and in the future.

You Can Posi-scan

To help build your faith in the Lord and your confidence in yourself as His special creation, I suggest that you learn to use what I call the "posi-scan" on your mental VCR. Use the "scan" button to scan back through all the positive things that have happened in your life. Be sure to use the *posi-scan* rather than the *negi-scan*. Think of answered prayers. Reflect on instances where you put your faith on the line, and God answered in a specific way. Remember how God has guided you, how He has blessed you in the past.

Think of your own successes, as well. As Christians, of course, we know that your personal successes are totally dependent on your Designer's faithfulness to you, and His grace and goodness toward you. For the moment, though, let's consider that important truth as being understood and accepted as a fact.

Now, flip back through your mental images of your own personal triumphs. The time you hit the home run in the championship Little League game, for instance. How about when you won the award for outstanding female vocalist? Or the time you aced that biology test.

Collect these positive images of past experiences and put them in your "Success" book, either literally or figuratively. Literally, you could start a journal of daily successes—not a diary of "poor, poor, pitiful me notes" written to yourself. In this journal write down specific instances where your prayers were answered or you scored some personal achievement. It will be a tremendously inspirational book to open on a sad and dreary day, when nothing seems like it's going your way.

Whether or not you choose to keep a literal success book, be sure to keep a mental photograph album with the images you want to remember. Allow only the positive pictures, or those negative images from which you have learned valuable lessons.

My wife, Angela, and I love to look back through our wedding album. It brings to mind such pleasant memories of our elegant wedding on Mackinac Island in northern Michigan. The album was created by master photographers David and Linda Smith of Stone Mountain, Georgia, who won an award for their outstanding efforts. The album was selected by the Professional Photographers of America as the best collection of wedding photographs entered into professional competition throughout the entire southeastern region of the United States for the year in which we were married.

As we flip back through the pages of this priceless compilation of memories, we have to laugh. The pictures are gorgeous! The people in the wedding party are all perfectly manicured and coiffed. The scenery at The Grand Hotel was breathtaking.

Nobody could tell from glancing through our wedding album, that the wedding was nearly a disaster. For one thing, the groom almost didn't make it to the church on time. In fact, I almost didn't make it to the *island* on time.

I had hired my good friend, Cal Kasparek, a Pennsylvania state trooper and an expert pilot, to fly the photographers, David and Linda, and myself to Mackinac Island. Angela, her family members, and my family were already there. We had planned on flying off into the sunset, following our wedding reception. What we hadn't planned on was Mackinac Island getting fogged in to the point that no planes could land on the tiny island.

When Cal and I left Pennsylvania on the morning of the wedding rehearsal, the skies were postcard blue. Not a dark cloud anywhere. By the time we reached Cleveland, however, where we picked up David and Linda, the skies had turned an ominous charcoal gray. As we flew northward, the weather grew increasingly worse. Our six-passenger plane was getting tossed about in the air like a Ping-Pong ball. Finally, after fighting the elements for several hours, Cal announced that we could go no farther. We had to go down, before we got knocked down.

We landed in the small town of Mount Pleasant, Michigan, still three hours away from Mackinac. Desperately, I tried to rent a car, but none were available. About the time I had almost given up hope, Roy Crain, a man I had never met before and have never seen since, came over to the phone and said, "I have a new Oldsmobile Cutlass Supreme. Take my car to your wedding!"

Overwhelmed by his generosity, but also cognizant that time was running out, we hurriedly thanked him and gave Mr. Crain seventy-five dollars for the "rental" of his car, and we were off again. Before leaving, though, I called Angela and told her to reverse the order of our rehearsal dinner and the rehearsal. It was already five o'clock and the rehearsal had been scheduled for six. "Go ahead with the dinner," I told her, and we'll have the rehearsal when I get there."

For the next three hours, we raced northward through Michigan, a cold rain pounding the windshield all the way. When we finally arrived in St. Ignace, the port from which we hoped to ferry across to Mackinac, the winds were whipping the water into lashing waves. As I stood outside at an unprotected pay phone, trying to get in touch with the wedding party, the rain was biting into my face like a thousand speeding needles. When at last I was able to get through to Angela's father, the news was not good. "Ken, the last ferry came over at five o'clock," he told me sadly, "and the next one won't run until seven tomorrow morning. I've checked with some of the local fishermen, and none of them will take a small craft out on the waters tonight. One of the best boat captains up here told me that this is the worst he's ever seen the waves on the lake.

"Ken, I guess you're going to have to stay over there tonight and try to get here as early as you can in the morning." Even the pounding, freezing rain couldn't conceal the salty tears that poured down my face, as I stood on the dock looking out into the black night. Somewhere, across the channel, my bride-to-be, our families, and the wedding party were preparing for our wedding—without *me!*

Several other things went wrong that are hardly worth mentioning: like the clock that never went off the following morning(fortunately, I was wide awake at 5:30 A.M.); like the circuits that blew out in my motel room as I was trying to get ready to catch the early-morning ferry; like the tuxedo trousers that were six inches too short (my brother Tink swapped with me, for which I will be forever grateful); like the weather that reminded us more of London than an island resort, like the golf ball that hit the roof of the church at a quiet point in the ceremony; oh, yes, there were a few other minor mishaps. But through it all, Angela and I got married, and through it all, David and Linda Smith created masterful photographs.

Now when Angela and I look back through our photo album, what do you suppose we see? Depressing photos? No way. Dreary, dismal weather? Not on your life! Through some photographic miracle, David and Linda produced photos that look as if they were done in a studio with controlled lighting. Every picture is part of a grand design, a story that the photographers were telling with the camera. When we flip back through those pages and recall the precious memories, it's almost easy to forget all the problems we had—*almost* easy!

Similarly, you can flip back through your positive impressions. For example, the next time you are assigned to make a speech in class, flip back through the images of all the successful speeches you have made. Don't dwell on the time the teacher called your name, and in your attempt to get out of your chair, you ripped the back out of your slacks. Don't dwell on the funny speech you thought you made, only to discover afterwards that your zipper had been down throughout your performance.

If you want to increase your confidence, scan back through some great speeches you have made. If you haven't made one, then make one now. You can make your speech to Mom and Dad, maybe your baby brother, or if nobody else will listen, make your speech to the mirror. Concentrate on how well you have done in the past, and it will give you confidence for the task you must do today, and faith to draw upon in the future.

In the same way, next time you want to ask that special someone out to the senior party, flip back to all the times your invitations have been accepted, not the one time you were told to drop dead.

When you want to share your faith in Christ with a friend, think back to the many times your witness has been positively received. If you've never had such an experience, then visualize an encounter in which you share your testimony, or what it means to be a Christian, with another person.

You can also use the process of visualization to see yourself as a better student, eager to attend class, better organized, being on time for school or work, and getting better grades.

Remember: you will move toward that which your self-image says you are, and that which you vividly visualize. Keep in mind, your images must be personal, practiced, and positive. One other important factor: be sure to *pray*. Ask your Designer to help you get the picture that He has of you and what He wants you to become. He wants much more for you than mere worldly success; He wants you to find true riches that will never fade away (*see* Revelation 3). Get His painting of you in mind, and keep it always before you. Then, start moving toward it, one step at a time.

Inside Out for
"What You See Is What You Get!"

1. *Think of an area in your life that you have difficulty over-coming or controlling. How could visualization, coupled with faith in your Designer, help you to win this battle?*

2. *What do you want to become in life? Is that how you see yourself today? How can you begin to think of yourself as more than a conqueror through Christ? Be specific!*

3. *Picture yourself as succeeding at whatever it is you want to do. Don't allow yourself to entertain thoughts of failure. Remember, your mind will attempt to complete the image in your mental VCR. What picture do you want your mind to complete?*

4. *When a negative thought or label comes your way, immediately think about something good or something positive, to cancel it out. Can you remember any negative thoughts or labels you have received recently? Practice visualizing a positive response and write it down.*

5. *Look up Romans 8:21. Read it out loud several times. How does that verse affect your attitude?*

6. *Read and memorize Philippians 4:13. This is one of the most powerful affirmations a Christian can make. What are some things that you want to do that will require you to trust Christ for special strength?*

7. *First thing in the morning, write a description of how you think your day will be. At the close of the day, jot down what actually occurred. How do the two lists compare?*

8. *Describe yourself as your see yourself today. Now, ask your Designer to raise that estimation by 10 percent. Where will that put you "tomorrow"?*

9. *Read Matthew 9:29 and Matthew 17:20. What does faith have to do with visualizing where you want to be?*

Where Are You Going?

10

*Do you know where you're
   going to?
Do you like the things that life is
   showing you?
Where are you going to?
Do you know?
Do you get what you're hoping
   for?
When you look behind you,
   there's no open door.*

Excerpt from "Theme From *Mahogany*" (Gerry Goffin and Michael Masser) © 1974 by Screen Gems EMI Music, Inc. 6920 Sunset Blvd., Hollywood, CA 90028. Used by permission. All Rights Reserved.

Perhaps no other song in the latter part of the twentieth century characterizes quite as accurately the pressing need of modern young people as does Diana Ross's poignant "Theme From *Mahogany*." Most high school and college students have virtually no idea of where they want to go in their lives, how they plan to get there, or how they will know when they have arrived at their destinations.

"What are you majoring in?" I asked a senior at the University of Hawaii.

"Elementary Education," she responded brightly.

"Wow! You must really love kids. What grade do you want to teach?" I queried.

"Oh, I'm not going to teach," she answered with a laugh. "And I really don't enjoy being around young kids all that much. Elementary just seemed like a relatively easy major; I had to pick something in order to get into a program, so that was my choice."

"Hmm," I pondered. "If you're not going to teach, and you don't like kids, what are you going to do when you get out of school?"

"Oh, I don't know," she answered airily, as if the thought had never occurred to her. "I guess I'll try to get a job somewhere. Maybe in the travel business."

Many young people don't *expect* to go anywhere in life, so they don't bother to plan or prepare. They are the floaters. Laid back on their rubber rafts, they are floating out to sea. Without a goal or direction, they are content to be controlled by the whims of the water and the wind. Naively, they are enjoying what they think is a free ride, oblivious to the fact that they are vulnerable to every violent change in the weather. They hope to end up on "Fantasy Island." More than likely, they'll soon find themselves in "The Twilight Zone"!

Traveling With an Empty Suitcase

It was a six A.M. flight to New York, and my eyes were barely open as I settled into my window seat aboard the softly lit jetliner. I was about to prop my pillow against the wall and try to get some sleep, when onto the plane walked a handsome couple decked out in party attire. She had on a slinky, sparkling-red evening dress, and he looked as if he had stepped out of the formal pages of *Gentleman's Quarterly*. On an early morning flight, filled with businessmen dressed in perfunctory blues, blacks, and beiges, this couple raised quite a few sleepy eyelids!

139

They excitedly made their way back to the aisle until they found their seats—right next to mine.

"Good morning," I offered tentatively, once they sat down. "My name is Ken Abraham." I extended my hand toward the man.

"Hi! I'm Bill. This is Jennifer!" he shook my hand vigorously as he spoke.

It was useless to ignore their unusual apparel and obvious early-morning enthusiasm, so I ventured, "Are you going someplace special today?"

"We sure are!" Jennifer chirped. "We're going to New York, and then we're going to catch a plane to the Bahamas. We won a three-day trip to Nassau last night!"

"Last night?" I repeated with a quizzical look on my face.

They both laughed hysterically before Bill finally regained his composure enough to say, "Yes. Last night! A local radio station held a promotional drawing at one of our favorite night spots. The only entrance requirement was that you had to bring a suitcase and be ready to go if you won. We didn't think we'd ever win, so we didn't pack anything in our suitcase. You can imagine how surprised we were when they called out our names!

"They whisked us off in a limousine for a late-night dinner at an expensive restaurant, then to a swanky hotel for a few hours' sleep, then off to the airport this morning. All we were allowed to take was whatever we had in our suitcase."

"Do you mean to tell me you don't have any clothes in your suitcase?" I asked, my mouth gaping.

"Not a stitch!" blurted out Jennifer, and they both began laughing uproariously again. "I do have my bathing suit. I put that in, just in case the judges asked to see something," Jennifer continued. "We just entered for laughs. We never dreamed we'd actually be going someplace."

"I guess we'll have to wear the clothes we have on our backs all three days," Bill contributed through tears of laughter. "I don't even have any money to buy anything once we get there."

"You don't have any money either?" For some reason, I started laughing myself, as I asked the question.

"Just what I had in my wallet when we went to the party," Bill answered more seriously. "We just didn't expect to be going anyplace, so we didn't pack anything. Nice joke, huh?"

Yep! Nice joke. Only for many modern young people, it is no joke. They live that way—not simply during a three-day dream trip. They operate day-to-day on the empty-suitcase principle. They don't anticipate going anywhere, so they don't pack anything in their bags. They don't plan, prepare, or propose any goals.

Other young people get easily sidetracked due to their lack of purpose. Cindy graduated from high school at the top of her class. She was bright, energetic, and excited about getting out into the real world. Jobs were tough to find, though, so when Cindy's friend Gail mentioned that the local factory was hiring, they both made a beeline to the employment office.

"We'll have a blast!" exclaimed Gail. "We'll get our own little apartment on the other side of town and live it up."

That is exactly what they did; they "lived up" their lives. They worked all week, and partied all weekend, squandering away their wages, their potential, and the years. At age thirty-five, Cindy is still working in the factory and paying for the apartment. Gail has long since gotten married . . . and divorced . . . twice, and Cindy is beginning to see the folly of an aimless life.

She said to me through her tears of regret, "Ken, I did more planning for the Senior Prom than I did for the rest of my life! I guess I expected all the pieces of the puzzle to come together by themselves. I thought maybe God or my parents or society would plan the parts of my life for me. Looking back, I can see that I didn't even have a proper picture of what the puzzle was supposed to look like."

Some people say they don't like to set goals or plan for their futures because it puts too much pressure on them. By not setting goals, however, they are literally abdicating the responsibility of their lives, giving it over to chance. As the saying goes, by failing to plan, they are planning to fail! J. C. Penney, founder of the department-store chain, once said, "Give me a stock clerk with a goal, and I will give you a man who will make history. Give me a man without a goal, and I will give you a stock clerk."

Should Christians Plan Ahead?

What about Christians? Should we meticulously draw up our plans and goals, or should we simply sit back with a fatalistic trust, hoping that everything will work out okay? Although it may seem absurd to you, some Christians are especially adept at spiritualizing their lack of goal setting and planning.

"Well, I'll just trust the Lord, and leave the planning up to Him," we often hear.

"God is in charge of my life, and if He wants me to get a college education, He'll be sure to let me know."

"The Bible says, 'Occupy until Jesus comes,' so I'm going to sit right here until He does."

Certainly, our trust must be in our Designer, not simply in our own wisdom, or our own abilities, plans, gimmicks, or success formulas. Nevertheless, while our God is committed to doing *His* 100 percent, He also expects us to use all the sanctified sense He has given us to do *our* 100 percent. Part of that entails planning, setting goals, and having a clear vision of our purpose.

Unquestionably, if your goals are intended for evil or if your plans are selfish in nature, you cannot expect the blessing and help of the Designer. He is more interested in your motivation than He is in your mere success. "All the ways of a man are clean in his own sight, but the LORD weighs the motives" (Proverbs 16:2). On the other hand, if your goals are godly and good, you can proceed with confidence. "Commit your works to the LORD, and your plans will be established" (16:3). Set your sights, plan your goals, but always remember, "The mind of a man plans his way, but the LORD directs his steps" (16:9). In other words, you may make the plans, but if they are to come about, it will be because your Designer is directing your steps.

The experience of Joseph is a good example of this. Acting upon the revelation he had received from God that a famine was coming to the land of Egypt, Joseph advised Pharaoh to tax the people 20 percent of the land's produce. This food, Joseph said, should be stored up for use during the tough times to come. Pharaoh thought it was such a splendid plan, he put Joseph in charge of overseeing its operation.

Probably a lot of Joseph's peers thought his planning was foolish and unnecessary. "Hey, Joe! What's the big idea! Why not live and let live? Relax. Take it easy. There's plenty of food. These are great days. Let's party! Eat, drink, and be merry for tomorrow we may die."

When the famine came, they were unprepared victims. They had failed to plan. But Joseph was unwilling to leave his future up to chance. He said, "This is the direction we are heading; here's how we're going to do it, and this is what we expect to happen." He combined his knowledge of the Word of God with good common sense; he saw what needed to be done, and initiated a plan of action designed to bring it to pass.

The apostle Paul was another planner. He was goal-oriented; he was not a wandering generality, looking for something to do with his life. He said, "I press on toward the goal for the prize of the upward call of God in Christ Jesus" (Philippians 3:14). Paul was not the kind of guy who could be content shuffling papers, trifling in trivia, majoring in minors, or indulging in mindless, tension-relieving activities. Can you imagine the great Apostle sitting at home every night, watching soaps or situation comedies?

On the contrary, he was a fierce competitor in the ultimate, all-or-nothing battle: the fight for the eternal souls of men and women. He could hardly believe that a Christian would allow

143

himself or herself to run a haphazard life for Christ. To the Corinthians, he wrote, "Do you not know that those who run in a race all run, but only one receives the prize? Run in such a way that you may win" (1 Corinthians 9:24).

Paul was never so headstrong about his own plans that he neglected the leading of the Holy Spirit. Once, when he and his party had planned to go into a place called Bithynia, the Spirit of Jesus did not permit them (Acts 16:6). Instead, the Lord led Paul to go into Macedonia. The Apostle changed his plans to coincide with the Lord's leading, and as a result, exciting new doors of opportunity opened in Paul's ministry.

Goal setting and planning also made sense to Jesus. When He was teaching about the exacting costs of discipleship, He asked the searching question, "For which one of you, when he wants to build a tower, does not first sit down and calculate the cost, to see if he has enough to complete it? Otherwise, when he has laid a foundation, and is not able to finish, all who observe it begin to ridicule him, saying, 'This man began to build and was not able to finish' " (Luke 14:28–30). In His own life, Jesus was constantly aware of the Father's plan. He knew His life was not an accident; He understood that the Designer had a purpose for His being here. Consequently, He lived His life on purpose. He knew where He had come from, what He was doing here, and where He was going. The night before the crucifixion, Jesus explained to His disciples, "I came forth from the Father, and have come into the world; I am leaving the world again, and going to the Father" (John 16:28). Because Jesus had His goal ever before Him, He would not be distracted or detoured—not by the clamoring masses, not even by His best friends.

A lot of Christians are reluctant to set goals because they are afraid of what it will look like if they fail. Said one youth leader, "I figured it would be bad enough if *I* set a goal and didn't make it, but if we set a goal as a youth group and didn't reach it, it would be a poor reflection on the Lord!" Though I appreciated his concern for God's reputation, I assured him that the Lord would rather the youth group attempt something great for God and fail, than to attempt to do nothing and succeed!

Solid Goals

What are goals anyhow? A goal is a purpose, an aim, a plan; it is something that, with your Designer's assistance, you expect to do. It is a statement of your faith; it is an expression of your belief in yourself and in God. It is like saying, "God, to the best of my knowledge and awareness, this is what I think You want me to do, and how I believe You want me to go about it. If I'm out of line, please show me. If I'm on target, please bless my best efforts."

It has been well established that the main reason for much of the juvenile delinquency in America is boredom. The main cause of boredom is a lack of goals. You have probably noticed the same phenomenon in your town. Two weeks after summer vacation begins, what is the most common statement among young people in your neighborhood?

"I'm bored!"

"What's there to do in this town?"

"Nothin' ever happens around here!"

Do you want to beat the boredom blahs? Then set some goals! Decide what you want to do, where you want to go, and what you want to be. Then formulate a plan as to how you can best get there.

How to Set Your Goals

In her one-woman show on Broadway, Lily Tomlin quipped, "I always wanted to be somebody. I see now that I should have been more specific" (*Life*, January 1986). Lily was right. The first and most important step toward *achieving* your goals is to be specific when you are *setting* your goals. Most people are much too vague about what they want.

The morning after a concert in Atlanta, Georgia, several members of ABRAHAM and a guest, who was traveling with us, stopped for breakfast at a restaurant that specializes in pancakes. ONE HUNDRED AND ONE VARIETIES OF HOTCAKES the sign along the road had touted the eatery.

"What can I get you to eat this morning?" asked the cheerful waitress, as we eagerly fingered the ten-page menu.

Our guest went first. "Oh, I think I'd like to have an order of pancakes," he answered thoughtfully.

I was afraid our previously cheerful waitress was going to feed him the menu as punishment for being so noncommital.

If you ever expect to reach your goal, you must define specifically what that goal is. It will do you little good to simply say, "I want to get rich," or "I'd like to get married someday," or "I want to lose weight," or "I hope to get more education," or even "I want to serve the Lord." Be specific! You need to focus on your objective and delineate it in as much detail as possible.

Recent research has confirmed that within your brain is a network of cells known as the "reticular activating system." It is the part of your brain that sorts out what is important to you. It is similar to a television antenna that pulls certain frequency signals out of the air and delivers them to your home screen. You decide which signals the reticular activating system will search for; you do this through your conversations and thought patterns, those things that you dwell on.

Whether or not those are important to the rest of the world makes no difference at all. Your reticular activating system is like a mental strainer that allows in only what it has been programmed to accept as important to *you*. Conversely, it will filter out anything deemed unimportant to you, regardless of its significance to others.

For example, the last time Steve Taylor or another of your favorite Christian artists was in town, your ears picked up on the announcement the first time you heard it. It was important to you, and your reticular activating system pulled in the information as rapidly as possible. On the other hand, did you notice when Isaac Asimov was lecturing at the university? Possibly so, but probably not, unless you happened to be tuned in to Asimov's work.

Your reticular activating system is running night and day, and based upon where you have centered your attention in the past, it accounts for what you will notice now.

On the ABRAHAM touring bus, my bed is located directly over the engine compartment. The first night we are on the road, I cannot sleep a wink. All I can hear is the roar of a huge, 318-Detroit bus engine beneath my pillow. After a few nights on the bus, however, I don't even notice the noise anymore.

One night, while we were working on an album in Chris Christian's Nashville studio, Chris was booked for a concert along with the guys who formerly made up the band "Fireworks." Since Chris was producing our album with us, we decided to take the night off and go along to the concert. Rather than take several vehicles, we all piled into our bus.

On the way back to Nashville, Chris slept in my bed. I tried to doze in one of the living room chairs in the front of the bus, while Brent Rowan, one of Nashville's top studio musicians, softly plucked his guitar in the chair next to me. When we arrived back at the Christian residence, I awakened the singer and asked him, "How did you sleep, Chris?"

"Okay, after a while," he replied, "but at first I wondered how you guys can sleep with all that noise!"

"What noise?" I asked.

"The noise from the bus engine," Chris replied.

"Oh, that! I didn't even notice that, but Brent picking that acoustical guitar all night about drove me crazy!"

Because your reticular activating system is programmable by your thoughts and conversations, it is important to concentrate on what you *want* when you are setting your goals. Once you have set the goal specifically in your mind, your self-image, along with your mental visualization computer and video recorder, and your reticular activating system all work together like the components in a guided missile aimed at a certain target. The reticular activating system will gather information and feed it into your mental computer; your self-image will analyze this information to see if it fits into your comfort zone. If all the results are positive, you will streak toward your goal, using the fastest and best route possible.

If your goal is not specific, you have about as much chance of reaching it as does a guided missile without a predetermined, particular target. It will proceed aimlessly, until it either runs out of power, hits an unfamiliar target, or self-destructs.

Does that sound like you or any of your friends? It certainly describes a lot of young men and women I meet. They are wandering aimlessly and erratically through life—accidents waiting to happen. If they have established any goals at all, they are usually ambiguous or nebulous, nothing that they can actually put any hooks into that will help pull them up the mountain.

Mel Fisher combined perseverance with his desire to reach a specific goal, and literally found himself a tub full of gold. Mel's gold was not at the end of a rainbow; it was fifty-four feet down in the ocean, forty miles off Key West, Florida.

For seventeen years, Mel Fisher searched for the wreck of the Spanish galleon *Nuestro Señora de Atocha*, which had sunk in 1622. Each morning as he and his crew searched the seas for the ship, Fisher encouraged his workers with the words "Today's the day." On July 20, 1985, it was! Fisher and his divers found forty-seven tons of silver and gold, a treasure worth over four hundred million dollars! Mel Fisher knew exactly what he wanted, and he would not give up until he had reached his goal.

Unfortunately, specific goals can work equally as well when they are set upon negative targets. If that is a beer party you are dwelling upon, your mental machinery will tune in every time your hear of one on campus. If it is a drug deal you are looking for, you will probably find it. If that is a lustful, premarital sexual escapade you are dwelling upon, your mind will help you develop your immoral, mental pictures.

Positively, if your goal is to be a starter on the varsity basketball team, or to sit "first chair" in the state concert band, your mind will aim at that target. If your goal is to learn one hundred verses of Scripture or to witness to fifty people this year, you will move toward your goal, if you continue to allow it to dominate your thoughts.

Once you determine what you really want, you will have made the most difficult and important decision in goal setting. Your Designer is specific concerning His plans for you. You be specific in your plans for Him.

Be a Realistic Optimist

Make sure your goal is large enough that it excites you, but small enough that it is within the scope of your imagination. A small, sure-thing type of goal won't get your adrenaline pumping. If your goal is merely to get through the day or to watch television half the night, you won't generate a great deal of initiative. Remember, we become what we think about; consciously or unconsciously, we are painting the picture we see in our minds. If your goal is simply to get by, to do enough work to pass the course, you are not going to be excited about going to school. If you put out enough energy to just barely make the team, you are not going to care whether the team wins or loses. If you merely want to be *just* another Christian musician, that's exactly what you will be. Set a big goal and go for it!

On the other hand, don't set your sights so high that you can't imagine yourself reaching your goal. Keep in mind that the concept of visualization will be important in your planning, and if your mind sees in advance that success is impossible, it will be.

Some people mistakenly assume that if a big goal is good, then a huge goal will be that much better. Wrong. If your goal is unrealistic or impossible to attain, the discouragement and frustration you experience by failing to see your plans come to pass may be counterproductive. Many people who set their initial sights too high—and fail—give up on planning and goal setting altogether.

"See! I told you all that nonsense about goal setting and planning would never work. You just have to accept life the way it comes to you."

Too bad. By setting their goals too high, they wiped out any chance of reaching a realistic goal. New Christians often get caught in this trap. When people first encounter Jesus Christ, they are so excited, they want to take on the entire world: "Let's see, I'm going to witness to ten people every day; I want to read twenty chapters of the Bible every day; I'm going to give half of my income to missions, and I will pray at least six hours each day!" No preacher or youth worker in his right mind wants to quell such enormous enthusiasm, yet if somebody doesn't attempt to funnel that energy toward realistic goals, the new believer can easily become disenchanted with the Church, disillusioned about other Christians, and discouraged in his or her relationship with God.

I recall hearing the late Keith Green say, "Don't ever promise the Lord that you will do *anything!* That's one of the most dangerous things you can do, as a Christian. Because then if you fail, you get tempted to give up." When I first heard Keith say that, I was surprised at his advice. As I reflected upon his words though, I understood what he meant. Many Christians bind themselves with ropes of their own making, like a little boy who keeps wrapping the garden hose around himself until he cannot move. As a result, these tied-up Christians are tormented by imaginary guilt for their imaginary failures, ineptitude, and ineffectiveness. Their conversation is riddled with statements like these:

"Boy, I should have done better today."
"I could have done that differently, if I had only used my head."
"If only I had said something else."
"I didn't get done what I wanted; I've failed again."

150

Before long, this kind of person frequently falls into the bondage of legalism in his or her Christian life. He or she can never quite do well enough; they can never reach the spiritual goals they have set for themselves, so they become locked into a system of *dos* and *don'ts*. "Do this and God will accept you; don't do that or your Designer won't like you anymore." They become the modern-day equivalent of the Pharisees of old—hard on themselves and even more critical and judgmental of others. They are often self-deprecating, fearful, worried, depressed, angry at God, and angry with themselves. This type of person is a prime candidate for a spiritual or emotional breakdown.

Don't set yourself up for guaranteed failure by setting your goals too high. The best goal is the one you place just beyond your current reach, but not beyond your imagination. Build up to bigger goals gradually. If you are making $3.75 an hour stocking shelves at the grocery store, don't set a goal of a million-dollar income next year! A goal of $4.25 per hour would be more realistic.

Let the accomplishment of smaller goals be faith-builders as you move toward larger goals. Rather than starting off by attempting to memorize entire books of the Bible, begin by learning one verse each day. If that is too much too soon, back off and attempt to memorize a verse every week. As you accomplish your goal, your confidence will increase and you will stretch your own limits further than you ever dreamed.

Inside Out for
"Where Are You Going?"

1. *Read Psalms 37:4, 5. How does this passage of Scripture relate to your goals?*

2. *What are some practical steps you can take toward reaching your goals?*

3. *When you complete every goal you have set, how will Jesus have been glorified?*

4. *Can you think of any persons from your graduating class who wasted away their potential? How did they do so? Why do you suppose they made the decisions they did?*

5. *What is the balance between planning your future and trusting God for your future?*

6. *If opportunity knocked on your door today, how would you be prepared to take advantage of it?*

7. *Read Daniel 1:17–20 and Daniel 2:19–23. How did God bless the plans of Daniel? When would intellectual planning be out of order?*

8. *What was the apostle Paul's favorite method of operation in taking the Gospel to new areas? Imagine a planning session with the great Apostle in which you are discussing how you can best reach your friends for Christ. What do you suppose his advice would be?*

9. *Read John 14:12–14. How will you know if your goal is too low?*

10. *List three tell-tale signs you are looking for to know that you have reached your goal.*

11. *One of the all-encompassing goals for every Christian is to see more people come to know Jesus Christ. What are you doing in your life today to help that goal become a reality? What can you do this year to be a better spokesperson for Christ?*

Blow the Lid Off Your Limits

11

Elephants are amazing creatures. When I was a child, I loved to go to the circus and sneak behind the big top to get an up-close view of the huge animals. I'd shut my eyes and imagine myself riding atop the magnificent beast, like Tarzan riding through the jungle.

I was especially fascinated by the way the elephants were restrained and tethered. Although my favorite circus animal had enormous size and strength, the trainer tied him up with a small, half-inch rope lashed to a stick only six to twelve inches long, which was driven into the ground. I was astounded! That ten-thousand-pound elephant could have pulled a truck down the road if he had wanted to, but he was held in place by a stake that was smaller than the ones Dad utilized to hold up his tomato plants.

One day, I asked the elephant trainer, "Sir, why doesn't he run away?" The trainer told me a fascinating story.

"Well, son," he began, "when Milton here was just a baby

elephant," he paused to stroke the leatherlike trunk of the elephant, "we had to tie him up with a heavy chain link, the kind you see on a construction crane. That chain was fastened to a six-foot pillar of steel and concrete buried in the ground, and we used heavy metal shackles on both ends. It wasn't that we wanted to be mean, it was just that young Miltie always wanted to run away, didn't you, Milton?"

The colossal circus creature swished his trunk back and forth, as if in agreement with the trainer. Milton extended his giant left foot and sent an ill-placed bucket of water sailing across the parking lot.

"Ha!" laughed the trainer. "See what I mean? Miltie can still be cantankerous if he wants to be."

I stepped back away from the elephant just in time, as the animal playfully twisted his trunk into a curlicue directly in front of my nose.

"Whew! Milton! You need a bath!' I said.

"Well, Milton kept right on trying to break away," the trainer continued matter-of-factly, "but he never could. One day, he quit trying. Ever since, all we've needed to keep him in his place has been this little stake. You see, son, elephants have excellent memories, and every time Milton thinks about breaking away, he remembers back to when he tried before and failed. So he doesn't even try. The trainer lowered his voice to a whisper, and turned away, as if he was trying to keep the elephant from hearing. "Son, you and I know that Milton could escape any time he wanted to, but he doesn't think he can, so please don't tell him any differently!"

Isn't that what many young people do to themselves? They see themselves as tied up, stuck in a rut. Consequently, they *are*. Unable to escape their memories of past failures, they have decided not even to attempt breaking out of the established patterns. They'd rather stay imprisoned in a cell of their own making.

Every once in a while, an especially courageous or rambunctious young man or woman will pull hard enough on the stakes so that they break free for a time. If they have no goals, however, where will they go?

Recently, I heard of an elephant trainer in Florida who has taken the tethering principle one step further. He has taught his elephant to *pick up* the small pup-tent size stake with which he restrains the huge animal.

He orders the beast, "Pick up the stake!" and the elephant dutifully pulls the small piece of wood out of the ground.

"Come over here," the trainer barks. Stake and all, the elephant lumbers over to where the trainer is standing.

"Now, put the stake back in the ground!" instructs the trainer.

Amazing as it may seem, the elephant buries the stake in the ground with his trunk, and he is *tied up once again!*

Couldn't the elephant figure out that if he moved the stake once, he could move it again? Of course, he could! Does he? Nope. He is chained to painful memories of his past performances.

If you ever hope to permanently escape the labels and limits of the past, you must make clear-cut, definite plans to do so, and then follow through on your goals.

Ask yourself some hard questions:

- What is your purpose?
- Where are you going in your life?
- What does it look like? feel like? sound like?
- How will you know when you have gotten there?
- Approximately how long will it take you to reach your goal?
- What do you regard as important steps along the way?
- Who is going to share this adventure with you?

Granted, most people never get this specific about their goals, and of course, that is one of the main reasons they accomplish so few of their aims. Your mind needs specific, clearly defined information if you expect your mental machinery to help you succeed in reaching your objectives. As such, I suggest that you write down the answers to the above questions as they apply to your spiritual life, your physical appearance and conditioning, your family responsibilities, your social life, your education, your financial plans, your professional and career goals, and your extracurricular or community activities. Take each one of these areas, ask yourself the hard questions, and write out the answers. It may take a little time, but I guarantee you, it will be well worth the investment.

Prioritize Your Goals

Another principle that will help you make definite plans for your future is to set a list of priorities for yourself. What is your overall game plan for life? If you have never thought about it, now is a good time to start!

"Aw, Ken, I'm only fifteen years old," objected a semi-serious, sophomore young woman. "What do I care about life-time goals? I just want to have some fun now!"

"That's terrific," I countered, "but when are you going to start working on your overall picture—when you're thirty? Why wait until a major chunk of your life is over and done with before you decide what you're going to do with it?"

Another question I ask young people is: "What do you want people to say about you when you are gone?" The answers run the gamut:

"That she was sexy."
"Oh, what an athlete he was."
"That I found a cure for cancer."
"That he was a nice guy."
"That she helped lead thousands of people to Jesus Christ."
"That he had the hottest wheels in town."

I also ask young adults, "If you went to the doctor, and he told you that you only had one year left to live, what would you do in these next twelve months?"

"I'd party, party, party!"
"I'd spend a lot more time praying and getting to know the Lord."
"I would travel as far as my money could take me."

Your answers to questions like these will go a long way in pointing out what you currently regard as priorities. The question you must then ask yourself is "Are my priorities in alignment with my beliefs?" For example, if you honestly believe that your Designer wants to use your life to spread His Word, what are you doing *right now* to make that a priority goal in your life?

In establishing a priority list for your goals, it will be helpful to break them down into categories. Start with your long-range, lifetime goals. What do you really want to do with your life? What do you regard as being of highest value to you. Are there some things that you would be willing to fight for? Sacrifice for? Even die for?

You'll find that once you establish your long-term goals, you are much less likely to be absorbed, overcome, or frustrated by the tyranny of the immediate. If you know where you ultimately want to go, you won't allow yourself to get bogged down by the fussers and whiners and the complainers. Ralph Waldo Emerson wisely pointed out, "The world makes way for the man who knows where he is going." On the other hand, as Robert F. Mager, author of *You Really Oughta Wanna* (Pitman), said with his tongue in his cheek, "If you're not sure where you are going, you're liable to end up someplace else."

Write It Down

After getting your long-term-game plan in mind, ask yourself where you want to be twenty years from now. Where do you want to be living; what do you want to be doing? Obviously, this is not going to be a static picture. You may change your twenty-year-plan every so often, as you experience new adventures in life and acquire fresh information. Nevertheless, it will help you to get an idea of what you are aiming at. Be as specific as possible. Don't just say, "Oh, I'd like to be a millionaire." Write out on a piece of paper what you will have done twenty years from now. Don't be afraid to dream lofty dreams. They are *your* dreams, not someone else's ideas of what they think you should be doing with your life, so don't allow false modesty or false humility to stifle your vision.

I suggest you do something similar in describing your goal for five years from now. Here, you can be even more specific. That horizon is not so far off. Is that a college education you see? Write it down! A house in the suburbs? Write it down. A talent, or a gift, or a ministry that you want to see expanded and put to better use for God? Write it down specifically, not simply in vague ambiguities.

Do the same thing for the next year. What do you hope to accomplish within the coming twelve months? Is that a new car you hope to buy? Write it down. Are you planning to try out for the school play or the church choir? Write it down. Do the same for your six-month goals, and your one-month goals. These short-term aims should be consistent stepping-stones toward your long-range goals. If they are not, then reevaluate their importance or, if necessary, adjust your long-term goals.

The most important goals you write down, however, will be your plans for each day. Keep a list of your daily priorities in a notebook or on a weekly calendar, or simply on a large writing pad. At the beginning of your day, write down (in a series of short statements) your list of things you want to do in that day. Carry over things that were not accomplished the day before.

Then, as you work down through your list of priorities, scratch off, or put a check by, each goal you have completed. Carry leftovers into tomorrow, and knock them off first thing in the morning. At first, this process may seem tedious and cumbersome, but after a short time, it will be second nature to you. Furthermore, you will be amazed at how much more you get done each day when you know what it is you want to do.

With all this talk about setting specific goals to be done within certain time frames, let me give you a word of caution: don't allow your growth to be inhibited by your artificial time frames. Growth takes time—and sometimes lots of it. Don't discard your goal simply because you didn't accomplish it within a given time frame. Simply adjust your schedule for the realization of your goal.

I once sat for over an hour in a 747 jet on the runway ramps of Chicago's O'Hare International Airport, as we awaited clearance to take off for Honolulu. It never crossed my mind to ring for the flight attendant and say, "This flight has been delayed. Let me off. The trip is not worth the wait!" On the contrary, I was willing to adjust my schedule because the destination was worthwhile, even if it meant not getting there as early as I would have preferred.

Some people allow time limits to scare them off from what they would like to do. A friend of mine complained, "Ken, I really hate my job!"

"Then why don't you try to get a different job?" I suggested.

"Oh, no! I couldn't do that," he exclaimed. "It's too late for me."

"What do you mean 'it's too late'?" I asked him.

"I can't change jobs this late in life. I mean, after all, I'm thirty-six years old!"

"So big deal! So you're thirty-six, so what? What do you want to be?" I pressed.

"Well, to tell you the truth," he dropped his eyes and hesitated before slowly and softly continuing, "I feel that God is calling me to be a preacher."

"Fantastic!" I burst out and began slapping him on the back. "That's great!"

My friend looked dismayed at my delight. "Ken, I can't be a preacher," he said dismally.

"What do you mean *you can't be a preacher?*" I practically shouted. "You just got done telling me that the Lord has called you to preach. Why can't you be a preacher?"

"I'm thirty-six years old, Ken."

"Yeah, I heard you before—so what?"

He seemed annoyed at my persistence. "Do you know how long it will take me to become a preacher? Why, I need four years of college, and then three more years of seminary . . ."

"Yes?" I urged him to continue.

"That's seven years! I'm thirty-six. Do you know how old I will be by the time I get to be a preacher? I'd be forty-three!"

"Oh! I see." I feigned a sudden enlightenment. "Hey, buddy. Let me ask you a question."

"Okay."

"How old will you be seven years from now if you *don't* become a preacher?"

"Forty-three," he answered quickly.

"Well, then, if you're going to be forty-three in seven years anyhow, you may as well go for it. Wouldn't it be better to be doing something you want to do, and something you feel God wants you to be doing, seven years from now, rather than being stuck in a job you hate, in a place where the Lord does not want you to be?"

"I never thought of it that way," he brightened.

Don't let time limits determine your goals. If your goal cannot be accomplished within your time frame, don't change your goal—change your time frame. Keep plugging! Success doesn't come overnight and rarely on your first attempt. Neil Simon wrote twenty-two full-length Broadway plays before he was finally honored with the prestigious Tony Award. As he accepted his award for "Biloxi Blues," at the 1985 awards presentation, Simon admitted, "I have always dreamed, naturally, of winning a Tony. I just didn't think I'd have to dream through twenty-two plays to get it" (*Life*, January 1986).

Silence Is Goal-Den

It is a sad commentary upon our society in general and upon our Christian community in particular, but you would be extremely unwise to share your goals with most people around you. Unfortunately, even in our churches we are surrounded by negative thinking, pessimistic cynics who will be glad to give you one hundred reasons why you will never reach your goal! In his popular book *See You at the Top* (Pelican), Zig Ziglar describes these people as having been "infected" by the world's most deadly disease: hardening of the attitudes, which is caused by stinkin' thinkin'! If you listen to them, you never will accomplish anything.

Losers and do-nothings will laugh at you for setting goals. Some of your less ambitious peers will put you down for planning your future, rather than committing it to fate. Misery always loves company, so don't be surprised if the lackluster and the lukewarm attempt to mock you into compromise. Your critics would like nothing better than for you to discard your Designer Genes heritage and return to the pigsty! They forget that while they are throwing dirt at you, they are simply losing more precious ground themselves.

I remember when I first decided I wanted to write a song. Some of my friends and relatives scoffed, "Ha! What makes you think *you* can write a song! What do you know about songwriting anyhow?"

"I don't know much," I confessed, "but I know enough to get started." To be sure, some of my early compositions were not classics—still, they were a start. I have now written over one hundred songs, with ideas brewing on several hundred more.

Straight Ahead

Have you ever tried to walk on railroad tracks? No, not at Grand Central Station, but have you ever tried to walk the tracks out in the country somewhere, where the trains seldom, if ever, run anymore?

My friends and I used to do it all the time, when I was about ten years old. I learned an important lesson walking those tracks: if you look down at your feet as you are trying to move forward, inevitably you will fall off. But if you keep your head up and your eyes straight ahead, you can go a long way before slipping, stumbling, or falling down.

Amy Grant has always been a girl with some big goals. At age twenty-four, all she wanted to be was "The USA's top pop singer with the wholesome image" (*USA Today*, September 12, 1985). But that hasn't kept both foes and friends from taking potshots at her. *USA Today* columnist Jack Kelly noted that "while her rock leanings have gained her greater commercial success, they've cost her some of her religious followers . . . in Detroit, fans presented her with a bouquet. Inside was a note: 'Turn back now. You can still be saved if you renounce what you've done.'"

Amy recalls: "'I cried in the shower, then went into the room and Gary [her husband] was in bed, and I said, 'Would you hold me for a while,' and I just cried. Gary prayed for us and then the words of my pastor echoed in my head, 'You are called to love them.'"

The title cut from Amy's best-selling album *Straight Ahead* sums up her attitude about goals and goons and goofs:

Straight Ahead

Day by day, dream by dream
I fight to find the way to go
Every day opens a different door
Every dream shadows the one before
But slowly I can see
The way You've made for me

Carry on through the night
When the road is hard to find
Lying lights tell me to turn around

Lying thoughts tell me I'm lost not found
But clearly I can see
You're waiting there for me

Straight ahead I can see Your light
Straight ahead through the dark
Straight ahead there's no left or right
Straight ahead to Your heart

Words and Music by Amy Grant, Gary Chapman, and Michael W. Smith. Copyright © 1984 Meadowgreen Music Co./Bug & Bear Music. Meadowgreen adm. by Tree Pub. Co., Inc., 8 Sq. W., Nashville, TN 37203. International Copyright Secured. All Rights Reserved. Used by Permission.

If you want to share your goals and plans with other people, be sure those people genuinely are interested and care about you. Or, you could run your goals by other people who are already succeeding at what you hope to do. For instance, if you want to be a dental hygienist, ask a professional hygienist to review your plans and your potential. If you want to be a professional Christian musician, attend seminars and conferences where other aspiring artists can share their achievements with you and vice versa.

Of course, there is one Person with whom you can share your most grandiose goal or most poetic plan, without fear of being laughed at, scorned, criticized, or otherwise degraded. His name is *Jesus*. And His plan for you is even grander than your loftiest goal. Don't share your dreams with duds. Share them with your Designer, and He will help you to complete the proper plan.

Revise Regularly

To be of real help to you, your goals should be updated on a regular basis. Some people like to do this on special occasions like New Year's Day or birthdays. Whatever you do, don't get hung up on a goal that is going nowhere. If your plan isn't taking you where you want to be, dump it! Formulate another plan of action. Ideas are expendable; life is not. If one idea doesn't work, don't keep polishing it and putting it on the top of your priority list. Let it alone. Maybe it's a good idea whose time has not yet come. Or maybe it's a lousy idea that you should flush at the earliest convenience. In any case, you won't know that unless you periodically evaluate your goals.

It is always a special time for me when I review my goals and see what I have accomplished, and how far I have to go. Often, I will set a predetermined reward for myself at the time I set my goal. If such incentives help you, give them a try. Your reward doesn't have to be expensive or exotic. It may be a special gift to yourself, something that you have wanted for some time but wouldn't buy under ordinary circumstances. Your incentive may be a special dinner, trip, or item of clothing that you've been thinking about. Be careful, though—as I mentioned earlier, if you don't keep your perspective, an incentive can become an albatross around your neck rather than a boost.

Keep in mind, too, that goals are not ends in themselves; they are a means to an end. They are stepping-stones to where you want to go. They are tools to be used to help you do the best with what your Designer has given to you.

Have you ever listened to the slogans that students toss around concerning their goal of graduation?

"It's time for kicks in eighty-six!"
"It will be like heaven in eighty-seven!"
"Just can't wait 'til eighty-eight!"
"We'll be done in ninety-one!"
"We'll be free in ninety-three!"

The juniors all say, "Boy, I can't wait 'til next year! Senior Power! Senior Privilege!" But then half-way through their senior year, what do you hear them saying?

"I can't wait to get out of this place and get a job."

We're like that, aren't we? We are goal-oriented by design,

but once we have achieved the goal, we are ready to move on to the next one. That should give you a hint about life: namely, if you simply concentrate on moving from goal to goal, you're going to miss most of the enjoyment of living. Don't be afraid to stop and smell the roses. Life is not a group of goals to be attained or designer labels to be collected. It is a journey, not simply a destination. Half the fun is getting there!

Goals are valuable, necessary, and good. But don't allow your goals to become your gods. Let God be God, and let your goals be means of glorifying Him as you live to your fullest potential.

Inside Out for
"Blow the Lid Off Your Limits"

1. *What would you like to see God do with your life within the next twelve months?*

2. *In what ways do you think the Lord can use you to be His representative?*

3. *Make a list of the goals you want to accomplish within the next twenty-four hours.*

4. *Read Psalms 90:17. Can you honestly pray this concerning your lifetime goals? Your twenty-year plan? Your five-year plan? Your one-year goals? Your monthly, weekly, and daily schedules?*

5. *Honestly explain why you are aiming at a particular goal.*

6. *Name three obstacles that must be overcome before you can reach your goal. Specifically, how do you plan to attack each obstacle?*

7. *What new information would better help you get to where you want to be in life? Where can this information be found? Do you know individuals who have already acquired this knowledge? How do you plan on getting the necessary information?*

8. *In Joyce Landorf's book* Balcony People *(Word), she says each of us has a group of people "cheering us on to victory." These are your encouragers, people who believe in your dreams, and in your goals. Name five people you would consider to be in your balcony (Don't forget Jesus!).*

9. *Industrialist Charles M. Schwab once said, "When a man has put a limit on what he will do, he has put a limit on what he can do." What limits are you currently placing upon yourself that your Designer wants you to break?*

10. *Memorize Luke 1:37. Let it be the standard by which you judge whether you can or cannot attain your goals.*

Talking to Yourself

The black van careens around the corner on two wheels, seemingly suspended endlessly in midair. Inside B.A. jerks on the steering wheel and the vehicle lurches onto all four wheels. "Face" and Murdock sit back and relax as "The A-Team" streaks away from the bad guys once again. In the co-pilot's seat, Hannibal reaches into the inside pocket of his jacket, pulls out a cigar, leans comfortably against the door of the van and with a mischievous twinkle in his eye, says, "I love it when a plan comes together!"

If your plans are going to come together, you must learn the principle of predicting and perpetuating your own positive performance! You can do this by discovering how to talk to yourself—properly.

"Oh, wow, man!" complained a nineteen-year-old fast-food restaurant worker. "Just what I need. I go around talking to myself all day as it is, and you want to teach me how to do it better?"

That's right! We *all* talk to ourselves all the time. Even

while you are conversing with someone else, or listening to a sermon, watching television, or reading this book, you are talking to yourself at the incredible rate of over a thousand words per minute. Until recently, however, relatively few people realized the potential these inner conversations held for altering personalities and performances. Not surprisingly, most of the individuals who understood the importance of their own mental chatter were extremely successful in their chosen professions. Soon others began to catch on to the concept that what we say internally, to ourselves, significantly impacts upon the way we live externally. As such, *self-talk,* the conversation you have with yourself, has become one of the hottest new buzz words of the eighties, and will most likely continue to be so in the nineties.

Unquestionably, your self-talk may well be the most important variable in all of the areas we have discussed thus far. What you say about yourself in your own mind will influence your potential, your self-image, your ability to visualize, and certainly the goals you set and attain.

Christians ought to be able to understand this principle even better than secular thinkers. We are conscious of the spiritual battle that is raging for the control of our minds. That is why the apostle Paul wrote, "We are destroying speculations and every lofty thing raised up against the knowledge of God, and we are taking every thought captive to the obedience of Christ" (2 Corinthians 10:5). We have learned the truth of "as he thinks within himself, so he is" (Proverbs 23:7), and we are aware that if a transformation is to come about, it must begin by the renewing of our minds (Romans 12:2).

Knowing all this, why then do we continue to talk dirty to ourselves? Stop and listen to some of the awful things you have been saying to and about yourself.

"I'm such a jerk."
"I never do anything right."
"If there is a way to mess something up, I'll find it."

"I can't stop smoking" (or drinking, or lying, or swearing, or doing drugs).

"I'm a lousy speller."

"My handwriting is horrible."

"I procrastinate all the time."

"I can't get along with other people."

"I hate myself!"

"I'm a poor student."

Imagine that you and your closest friend are walking down the street together, when suddenly, for no reason at all, your buddy begins punching you in the stomach with all his might. Then, while you are doubled over in pain with the wind knocked out of you, he knees you in your nose. You fall to the ground, writhing in agony, and he begins to kick you and jump up and down all over you.

"Wait a minute!" I hear you shouting. "With friends like that . . ."

You are absolutely correct! Yet that is precisely what many people do to themselves. Through negative self-talk, they repeatedly beat up on themselves, and then, masochistically keep coming back for more. They harangue themselves with all sorts of despicable and demoralizing labels.

"What a klutz I am."

"You lamebrain."

"Way to go, moron!"

"Dummy! Stupid! Motormouth! Worthless! Atta-boy, bonehead! What a nerd you are! You gross ogre! Fat slob!"

There's Some of Ed in All of Us

It is early on "The Tonight Show," and Ed McMahon and Johnny Carson are bantering back and forth at Johnny's famous desk before the other guests are introduced. Ed begins to set up a comedy bit for Johnny, and we can almost sense what is coming. As Ed's voice increases in volume and intensity, we chuckle knowingly. "That's absolutely amazing," exudes Ed. "To think that everything we'd ever want to know about [whatever] is right there on that paper!"

"You're wrong, buffalo breath!" cracks Johnny, and the studio audience laughs hysterically, as do millions of viewers at home.

But have you ever asked yourself, *Why am I laughing at another person's being called* buffalo breath? Perhaps it is because we can identify with poor, put-upon Ed. We sometimes feel like buffalo breath and yak noses and camel ears ourselves. Similarly, we identify with Rodney Dangerfield when he laments, "I don't get no respect!" We empathize with Phyllis Diller, as she makes a living by putting herself down. We laugh with Don Rickles and Joan Rivers as they slice other people apart through their use of scathing and sarcastic labels. It's all in good fun, but deep down, oftentimes, we feel the joke is on us!

Undoubtedly, that is also one of the reasons why America identifies so well with Charlie Brown of the comic strip *Peanuts*. Charlie has a hard time feeling good about himself. Consequently, his self-talk is usually negative. He is constantly the victim of self-criticism and is often the goat for somebody else's joke. He sounds a lot like some of us.

Putting on the Right Labels

The labels you wear on your jeans aren't nearly as important as the labels you place upon yourself through your self-talk. The words you use to describe yourself will be manifested in the things you say and do.

When Curt is having a bad day on the tennis court, you better watch out, and plug your ears. "Nice shot, wimpy." "Keep the ball in the court, will you?" "Does your mother play? She could certainly do better than you." "You imbecile." "Come on, jerk, can't you offer some competition?" "You limp-wristed baby!"

And these are the things Curt says to *himself*. No wonder he is frustrated in his game. He is talking himself right off the court. If he wants to improve his tennis, he needs to start by improving his self-talk.

I was explaining this principle to my nephew, Eric, on the golf course one day. Both of us were hitting the ball poorly and frequently, and Eric was becoming more frustrated and angry with every shot.

"Nice going, you moron," he said to himself after a particularly bad shot.

"Eric, don't say that," I cautioned. "You are not a moron. You are intelligent, handsome, kind, sensitive, strong, generous, and an all-round decent guy. On top of all that, you're a pretty fine golfer!"

"Yeah, well, thanks," Eric blushed self-consciously, "but what are you supposed to say when you hit a crummy shot?"

"Say, 'That sure wasn't like me.' Tell yourself, 'I'll do better next time. That was a poor shot, but the next one is going to be right where I want it!'" I encouraged him.

We both took our next shots, and promptly blasted two beautiful golf balls into oblivion, somewhere in the deep, dark "black hole" known only to golfers who are having bad days. Up and down the fairways, you could have heard, "That's not like me! That's not like me!"

"Me neither!"

Write Your Own Ticket

How, then, do you go about restructuring your self-talk and putting proper labels on yourself? The key to internalizing a goal or a statement about yourself, is to *describe yourself as though you had already achieved it*. I suggest you do this by writing out your goals or affirmations and rereading them daily. Get yourself some three by five cards and for each goal, write at least one statement describing it on a card. These reminders must be positive, personal, and in the present tense.

Write your affirmation in a *positive* way. It won't do you

much good to write, "I want to stop being late for class or for work." You need to write, "I am proud of myself for being on time at school [or work]." (Notice: you are writing this goal as if it is already a *reality* in your life.)

Similarly, your statements must be *personal*. Use personal pronouns *I, me, my,* and *mine* when you are affirming your goal. A statement like "Organized people get better jobs" won't help you reach your goal of being better organized. You must write on your card, "I feel good about being a consistently well-organized person."

Notice, too, that these flash-card affirmations must be in the *present tense*. Write out your goal as if you are enjoying it right now, this very moment. Don't write your goals in terms of *someday, maybe,* or *"if I'm lucky."* Don't write it in a future tense, as something you hope you will be doing. Write it as if you have already achieved the goal, and it is a present tense reality in your life. Even "dream goals" should be put into the present, not in the future. Don't say, "Someday, I'd like to take a Caribbean cruise." Put it this way: "I enjoy sunbathing on the Promenade Deck of my cruise ship enroute to Ocho Rios."

If you want to play par golf, write: "I feel fantastic because I'm regularly shooting golf in the low seventies."

If you are never prepared for class, but you want to be, write it down positively: "I enjoy preparing for class daily." "I enjoy participating in classroom discussions" might be another affirmation you will want to try.

If you want to be an effective public speaker, don't simply say, "I want to make good speeches." Say: "I enjoy having a witty, warm, yet authoritative public-speaking manner."

Try to make your affirmation as specific as you can by using numbers or descriptive phrases whenever possible. You will be better off, however, if you avoid using categorical or exclusive words such as *always, every day,* and *never*. Replace them with strong habitual words such as: *regularly, readily,* or *consistently*. Unless you are a robot, nobody *always* does what he or she wants to do! Don't shoot for perfection; just shoot for improvement.

These flash cards are for your eyes only. You shouldn't share this information with anyone else, unless you feel strongly that they are in your corner, or will be intimately involved in the achievement of your goal. You are not in competition with anyone but your own best self, so don't compare yourself with other people. For instance, there is no need to write, "I will lose more weight than Mary." If you want to lose weight, write down what you want to weigh. "I enjoy weighing one hundred twenty pounds and working out at the racquet club regularly."

Some other examples of positive goal affirmations are:

- I enjoy being an aggressive rebounder, going up in the crowd and ripping the ball off the boards.

- I feel fabulous in my new suit.

- I enjoy singing on pitch before a large, enthusiastic crowd.

- I regularly finish whatever task I begin.

- I consistently budget my time and money well.

- I readily express my feelings to my family and loved ones.

- I am in control of my diet.

- I enjoy having a 3.5 grade point average.

Who's the Boss?

"But these are only words," you may object. "What good are a bunch of words? Words aren't worth anything!"

Ahhh, that is where you are wrong. Words have a life and a power all of their own. You can never erase the negative words that have seeped into your subconscious mind and have lodged in your self-image. You may not be able to remember them, but they are there. It is impossible to wipe them out. You can, however, overcome the negative inputs you have received in your life by programming your mental computer with positive, purposeful data. Your Designer will use your positive visualizations along with your goals and positive affirmations to redesign your self-image. Your self-image will then have a direct effect on how you live on a day-to-day basis.

"But these affirmations aren't even true!" you might say. They don't have to be; not at this point, anyhow. We are affirming what you *want* to be, not what you *are* right now. We're talking about where you want to go, making fullest use of your Designer-given potential. Some people call it a positive confession. I simply call it *faith*.

Now It's Your Turn

Once you've written out your flash cards, the next step is to start using them. Try to find a few minutes every morning when you can sit down and unwind. In a relaxed atmosphere, simply read through your flash cards. You may want to play some soft music as you read them, but don't allow the music to distract your concentration. Try to visualize your goal as you read each one. Picture it in your mind. Feel it! Experience it with your senses. Remember, visualization must be in the first person; you must sense the experience as if it is happening to you. See it through your own eyes, not the eyes of someone watching you from the bleachers.

For example, if your goal is to take the Gospel to the mountains of South America, first of all, write on your flash card: "I am thrilled at how God is using my life to bring more South Americans into the Kingdom of heaven." As you read your goal each morning, picture yourself learning the language and sharing the Gospel with the native people. Feel the weather, the heat or the cold; sense the smells of the foods in your future mission post. Feel the ground beneath your feet as you travel through the mountains, taking the Gospel to another person.

Read these flash cards every morning and every evening, or

any time when you can relax and concentrate upon them. Don't get too many cards, but you should be able to handle five or ten at each reading. As you accomplish your goal, file away the appropriate card so you can bring it out at a later time, as a faith-builder and as a reminder of past victories.

If your cards are not available, you can still practice in your mind. Rather than wasting time standing idly in a cafeteria line, or waiting at a drive-thru, concentrate upon your goal.

Tape a written reminder on your mirror. Jot your affirmation on your doodle pad, next to the telephone. Scribble it on the backs of envelopes. Put a note on the refrigerator. Put it anywhere that is helpful to you—and legal! You will remember, won't you, that custodians frown upon even the grandest goal-reminder if it is carved into a desk or written on a restroom wall!

One more thing: don't forget to pray regularly over your plans, goals, and aspirations. Prayer is the power that pulls all of your efforts together into the Designer's master plan. As you pray, you may discover that some of your plans and goals are inconsistent with His plans and goals for you. If so, don't waste your time trying to talk Him into seeing things your way. Align your goals with His will for your life, and you can't go wrong! "Faithful is He who calls you, and He also will bring it to pass" (1 Thessalonians 5:24).

Inside Out for
"Talking to Yourself"

1. *Set three new lifetime goals and begin to pray specifically that the Lord will bring them about in your life.*

2. *Name five ways you have grown to be a better person in the past year.*

3. *What area of your life needs the most change during the next year?*

4. *Why should you not compare yourself with others?*

5. *Make a conscious effort to rid your vocabulary of such phrases as "I have to," "I can't," "I should have," "I don't have any choice," and "I wish I could."*

6. *Begin using phrases like: "I choose to," "I am going to," "I'd like to," "I want to," and "I have decided." Try to create five situations in which you can use one of these expressions.*

7. *How can you better set your own standards, rather than comparing yourself with someone else?*

8. *When you do something out of character, remind yourself, "That's not like me." What does that do to your self-image?*

Do You Want to Get Better?

13

And a certain man was there, who had been thirty-eight years in his sickness. When Jesus saw him lying there, and knew that he had already been a long time in that condition, He said to him, "Do you wish to get well?"
John 5:5, 6

When I first read the account of how Jesus dealt with the fellow who was lying at the pool of Bethesda, I thought, *Wow, Jesus! What a cruel thing to ask a guy who has been sick for thirty-eight years!* "*Do you wish to get well?*" After counseling with thousands of teenagers and young adults over the past eighteen years, however, I have come to conclude that Jesus' question was poignantly accurate and a precise, psychologically sound analysis of the situation.

The big question for most of us is not "Can you be made well?" It is "Do you *want* to be better?" Do you genuinely wish to become a whole person, or would you prefer to continue life as a spiritual and emotional cripple?

Most of us have enough head knowledge to be well. We have been inundated by sermons, tapes, books, and a plethora of other self-help aids. If a person is honestly looking for some answers, he or she will have little trouble finding them.

Neither is the question, *can* Jesus make us well? Nor is it, do we have enough spiritual, educational, or financial resources? Are there competent counselors available from whom we can draw strength? All these questions are superfluous. Jesus put His finger right where the real problem lies: "Do you wish to get well?"

Patti approached me at "Jesus 85," a major Christian festival held each year in Central Pennsylvania. Patti is a perennial problem. She doesn't just *have* a problem, she *is* one. This year Patti's timing was impeccable—impeccably poor, that is! I was hurriedly wolfing down an order of French fries on my way back to the bus, just prior to ABRAHAM's performance—with no time to lose—when she stopped me on the road.

"I'm going to commit suicide," she stunned me with her words. I nearly choked on the French fry I was swallowing.

"You're *what?*" I finally managed to ask, after a few gulps of coffee.

"Yep. I'm gonna do it this time. I've tried to slit my wrists before. Here, look at them," she thrust her arms in my direction, as she continued, "but I never had enough guts to do it. This time I'm going through with it. Nobody cares about me. My friends don't care. God doesn't care. The people I came here with don't care. You don't care. Why should I? I'm just going to end it all."

"Hey, hang on, Patti!" I shouted at her. "Slow down, and tell me what's the matter." Patti and I had talked about her "problems" several times before, and by now, I could be direct with her.

"It's my friends," Patti began again. "Or, at least, the people I thought were my friends. They don't want to hang around with me. They tell me I'm not concerned about being a

Christian. I'm just a groupie following after all the musicians."

"Well, are they right?" I asked her.

"No!" Patti responded emphatically.

"What else?" (There was always *something else* when I talked with Patti.)

"They say I'm ugly, that I'm dirty, that I never clean up. One girl even told me to go take a shower. She said my hair looks like someone poured axle grease on it."

I took a look at Patti. She wasn't ugly, but she was quite crusty. "Well, maybe your friends have a point, Patti," I said gently. "Maybe you ought to clean yourself up a bit. You are an attractive person. If you'd just take care of yourself, I'll bet you would feel better about yourself. And you'd be more comfortable around your friends, too."

"Baah, you are just like all the rest of them," she retorted. "Just pray for me, will you? I don't really want to commit suicide, but sometimes, I sure feel like I'd be doing the world a favor if I did!"

"Okay, Patti. I'll pray for you, but I'm not going to let you off the hook so easily. You know the Bible as well as I do. It's time you start living the way God wants you to; quit messing around with the booze and the drugs and always feeling sorry for yourself."

"Just pray, will you?" Patti responded impatiently.

"Sure, I'll pray," I answered, "but you are going to have to start doing some things on your own, too. Start reading your Bible, and talking to the Lord, and start going to church, too."

"Yeah, yeah; I will. I promise, Ken."

I prayed for her, right there on the road, then we went our separate ways. I knew she wasn't going to commit suicide, but I also knew that she had no intention of changing. She didn't *want* to be made well.

Do Something Now!

Two things are necessary if you want Jesus to heal you and put you back together spiritually and emotionally. One, you must let go of the sins of the past, your failures, your mistakes, your rebellion against God's will for your life. Two, get up; start trusting Jesus at His Word, and start walking with Him.

It is precisely at the first point, however, that many people miss out when they are seeking to repair a damaged self-image, or to redirect their lives in a positive direction. For many individuals, it is not Mom, Dad, or Freud, that binds them to the past. It is unforgiven sin. Most secular, humanistic, self-help programs don't talk much about sin. Unfortunately, many modern-day Christians don't either. That prompted medical doctor and theologian, Karl Menninger, to call for a renewed emphasis on the real problem in his provocative book *Whatever Became of Sin?* (Hawthorn).

It is almost unbelievable how many people will hang on so tenaciously to the thing that Satan uses to make them sick, and to turn their lives upside down. Although they talk a great deal about wanting to be well, they continue to hold on to past sins.

When I was a teenager, I had a dog by the name of Nipper. Nipper was a German shepherd-collie, a beautiful dog, but not too bright. Nipper was, however, an extremely playful pooch. He would often bring my leather jacket to me and bark until I compliantly took one end. He would then hang on for dear life, as I'd swing both jacket and dog around in circles. Around and around he would fly, clutching the jacket with his teeth. Faster and faster he'd whirl, his eyeballs looking as if they were turning somersaults in his head! Finally, just on the verge of getting sick, he'd let go of the jacket and roll off into a corner of the house. The next day, he'd be right back, barking for more of the same.

Many people who suffer with intense depression and self-esteem problems are similar to Nipper. They keep on hanging on to the very thing that is causing their ailment. Often it is a sin from the past. Sometimes it is a sinful action or attitude in the present. Regardless, if that is you, don't lie with the sick folks any longer. Get up and trust Jesus with your life. Quit making excuses for yourself! Stop feeling sorry for yourself, or pouting in self-pity. If you will say, with a conscious act of your will, "I am going to trust Jesus," you *can* be made whole, spiritually and emotionally, and perhaps, physically as well. The only thing for which Jesus waits is the consent of your own human will.

We don't expect a supernatural God to work that way, do we? We expect Him to grab us by the hand and yank us to our feet. But our loving Designer doesn't do things like that. He will provide the *power* for you to get up, but you must have the *will*. You must have the *desire*. You must have the *faith*.

Excuses, Excuses

Jesus stood above the man who had been sick on his bed for thirty-eight years and asked him, "Do you want to be made well?"

You would expect the man to have accepted Jesus' offer immediately, and cried out, "Oh, yes, Lord! I do want to be well. I've been waiting for so long. My need is so deep. I've been hurt so badly. I'm sick and I'm tired, and I'm sick and tired of being *sick* and *tired!* I don't want to live in this defeated, crippled condition any longer."

That's what you and I would expect the man to do, right?

But he didn't. If you read the entire account, you will discover that he did what many modern-day spiritual and emotional cripples do when confronted with an opportunity to get well. He began making excuses for his decrepit condition.

First of all, he said, *"I'm waiting."* He was waiting for the moving of the waters. Tradition had it that "an angel of the LORD went down at certain seasons into the pool, and stirred up the water; whoever then first, after the stirring up of the water stepped in was made well from whatever disease with which he was afflicted" (v. 4).

We are such terrible procrastinators, aren't we? We wait until everyone else starts moving, then figure that we will join the crowd. "When my boyfriend becomes a Christian, then I will too." "When everyone else in my young adult group gets excited about Jesus, then I'll join them."

Perhaps you feel you ought to become a better Christian; or maybe you know that you need to allow the Holy Spirit to have full control in your life; or you say, "I want to deal with this self-esteem problem"; or "I'm going to start living up to my potential"; or "I want to start setting and attaining some goals . . .

"But not today. I'll start *tomorrow*."

You know as well as I do, *tomorrow never comes!* Satan loves to help you put off until tomorrow what you know you should do today. No wonder the apostle Paul wrote, ". . . we also urge you not to receive the grace of God in vain—for He says, 'At the acceptable time I listened to you, and on the day of salvation I helped you'; behold, now is 'the acceptable time,' behold, now is 'the day of salvation' " (2 Corinthians 6:1, 2).

If you wait until you are ready, you may never get ready! How many miserable old bachelors do you know who decided to wait until they were ready before they got married? How many losers do you know who say, "One of these days, when I get good and ready, I'm going to straighten out my life"?

That's part of the problem. When it comes to having faith in Jesus, you can't get good, and there is really nothing you can do to get ready. He simply asks you to trust Him. *Now.*

The man's second excuse was *"I've tried before and failed."* He said, "I've been sitting here for thirty-eight years. I've seen the waters stirred before, and I've tried to make it, but couldn't." Perhaps, you too are saying, "God has spoken to my heart before about some of these areas, and I have honestly tried to get into a relationship with Christ; I wanted to be healed of my spiritual and emotional maladies, but I couldn't get it together. I kept messing up." The Good News is, "If we confess our sins, He is faithful and righteous to forgive us our sins and to cleanse us from all unrighteousness" (1 John 1:9).

Mylon LeFevre must be the "comeback Christian" of the

eighties. As a child, he was surrounded by Christian influences. His grandfather was a preacher, and his mother and father were the leaders of one of Christian music's original dynasties "The LeFevres." But being a successful gospel musician wasn't satisfying to young Mylon, and it became even less so when Elvis Presley recorded "Without Him," one of Mylon's early attempts at songwriting.

"My first royalty check from 'Without Him' was for ninety thousand dollars!" Mylon told me, as we swapped stories on our bus after a concert we had done together in Erie, Pennsylvania. "What in the world was a seventeen-year-old kid like me going to do with ninety thousand dollars? One of the first things I did was to go out and buy a car, a fancy Corvette, and I paid cash for it."

The allure of riches, fame, and drugs appealed to Mylon, and before long he became known as the rebel of "The LeFevres." But Mylon was moving too fast to worry about that. He was performing with some of the top names in secular music, names like Eric Clapton, George Harrison, and the Atlanta Rhythm Section. Everything that Satan could offer a young man was at Mylon's fingertips, and the guitar-playing singer reached for it all.

It wasn't until Mylon LeFevre realized that the devil was killing him with "success" that he was able to return to the Lord, almost twenty years later. At first, many of Mylon's friends and relatives didn't believe he had been converted. Many Christians were suspicious of the long-haired, rabble-rouser-turned-disciple, much the way the early disciples were cautious about receiving a former persecutor of the Church, named Paul.

But Mylon's conversion proved to be genuine. He walked away from life in the fast lane and decided that he was going to follow Jesus, even if it meant sweeping floors for a living.

It did. "Ha! I was making six hundred thousand dollars a year about the time I met Jesus," chuckles Mylon. "When I walked away from that, I didn't know *how* I was going to survive. Most of the Christian folks I knew didn't want anything to do with me, and when I got saved, my rock music buddies cut me off cold. They said, 'Mylon, you done flipped out!' So I took a job as the church janitor at Mt. Paran Church of God in Atlanta. Those people gave me a chance; they took me in and loved me, just the way I was."

This time, things were different for Mylon. "I had tried, man. I had tried real hard to be a Christian before. But now, there was a hunger in my heart for God. I wanted to know Jesus better, so I hung out at the church a lot. I talked to people who knew Him well, and I prayed that He'd give me another chance."

Musicians gravitated to the former rock star and before long, Mylon was playing music again, only this time, the music was for Jesus. As Mylon grew stronger in his faith, the music ministry continued to expand, first at Mt. Paran, then to all Atlanta, then throughout the United States. His group "Mylon LeFevre and Broken Heart" still uses all the ingredients of a heavy-duty rock show, but the ministry has been instrumental in bringing thousands of young people to Jesus. Mylon LeFevre has come full circle.

Other people was the third excuse the lame man in John 5 used to rationalize his condition. When Jesus asked him if he wanted to be well, he complained, "Sir, I have no man to help me" (*see* v. 7).

Maybe that's been your excuse, too. "I've wanted to serve Jesus, but other people have let me down. It would be a wonderful world, if it just wasn't for all those *other people!*"

A friend of mine is a musical genius. He is a veritable fountain of creative ideas, a man whose abilities have been recognized and honored throughout the professional music industry. It is doubtful, however, that you will ever see my friend appearing on one of the annual music awards shows, although he could be there if he so desired. Unfortunately, he doesn't like to be around people. He feels that they have all done him dirty, or would if they could. He is certain that somebody is out to get him.

Consequently, my friend won't take part in any of the promotional activities that could enhance his career. He is convinced that he has been victimized by the system. He has been burned before, and he is not going to stick his neck out again.

If that sounds like you, you need to realize that *everybody* has been let down by *somebody*! Furthermore, every one of us has disappointed someone else, at some point in our lives. It is irresponsible to say, "My preacher let me down," or "My boyfriend [or girlfriend] betrayed me," or "My youth leader disappointed me." Each one of us is accountable for our own actions and our own *responses* to the actions of other people. You may not be able to control what other people say about you, or do to you, but you alone decide how you will react. You can clam up in your shell, or you can trust your Designer to bring you out on the positive side of life.

In addition, look to Jesus as your security. Decide in advance, that no matter what anyone else says or does, you are going to stick close to Christ. "For the Scripture says 'Whoever believes in Him will not be disappointed'" (Romans 10:11).

The man's final excuse was a familiar one: *"I'm inferior."*

He cried, "I can't make it on my own! I'm not as strong as everyone else. You have to understand, Jesus, when the waters are stirred, it's not that I don't want to go; I do. Honest, I do! But I'm not able. Someone else always gets there before I do."

Does it sound like this fellow was reading from your diary? "Others can make it, but I can't. Maybe Bruce or Shelly can live for Jesus but I'm just a filthy sinner. Always have been; always will be, I guess. I know my place in life; this is where I'm at, and this is where I have to stay.

"Others are more talented than I am. They have such pleasing personalities, and such incredible physical abilities and mental aptitudes. But when the gifts were handed out, I didn't get any."

185

Designer Genes

Diana and the Specialist

When Diana Hegedus was born, she was a lovely, cherublike baby. Overjoyed at this precious gift of new life, Bob and Shirley Hegedus took their daughter home to raise.

Diana did fine until she was five years old. Then one morning, the normally pleasant-tempered Diana woke up screaming! Her parents rushed to her room, and found, to their horror, that Diana's leg had bent completely backward and would not straighten out! They tried everything they could think of in their attempts to release Diana's leg, but it remained rigid. Frantically, they called the doctor and rushed Diana to the hospital.

At the hospital, the doctors immediately set about conducting a series of tests on the little girl. Though in strange surroundings and in intense pain, the frightened child was a model patient. She didn't understand what the funny-sounding words meant when the doctors reluctantly diagnosed her condition as "rheumatoid arthritis." All she knew was that she had to go in for therapy three times every day, and take handfuls of aspirins. Oh, yes, there were those awful series of gold shots.

As Diana grew older, the debilitating disease continued to rack her body with pain. When she was in second grade, she fell off her bicycle, and chipped a tooth. As a result of her fall, Diana's fragile mouth began to curl uncontrollably.

More than three hundred doctors at the University of Pittsburgh studied Diana's case and declared it was hopeless. Her teeth were over one hundred degrees out of chewing alignment, and her hands were becoming more deformed by the day. There was nothing to do but watch and wait as Diana's body literally disjointed itself out from under her.

Diana, however, knew a specialist who most of her doctors didn't; Diana knew her Designer! When the doctors said she must submit to the surgeon's knives, Diana was undaunted. Her spirit was indefatigable as the orderlies wheeled her toward

186

the operating room. "It's okay, Mommy," she said from her prone position on the gurney, "don't cry. I know that Jesus will take care of me."

And He did! Doctors have proclaimed Diana as a walking miracle. Diana remains handicapped, but she is certainly not crippled! Other people have tried to discourage her by telling her what she *cannot* do, but Diana refuses to accept their negative input. She has discovered that the combination of faith in her Designer, and self-determination will take her wherever she wants to go. Those legs that the doctors said would never hold her, have carried her to such exotic places as Hawaii and Jamaica. The body that negative-thinking pessimists said would never function, swims in her own pool every day the sun shines. The fingers and hands that cynics said would soon cease to move have mastered an IBM computer system, and have typed every single word of the manuscript for the book you hold in your hands!

Diana is an inspiration in many ways. One of Diana's friends said to her, "Diana, I know you are handicapped, but I see something in you that I need. I want to know what you are made of. Whenever I look at you, I see Jesus!"

You don't have to simply accept life the way it comes to you. Your Designer is ready and willing to make the necessary alterations. All it takes is a little faith on your part.

Notice how Jesus responded to the lame man's objections. He didn't argue with the sick fellow; He didn't try to point out the areas in which the man had painted an unrealistic picture of his condition. No, Jesus went straight to the heart of the matter. He brushed aside all of the man's excuses as if to say, "I don't want your excuses; I want your will!" He stood directly in front of the man and commanded, "Arise, take up your pallet, and walk" (v. 8). Something supernatural happened right there on the spot. "And immediately the man became well, and took up his pallet and began to walk" (v. 9).

I truly belive that Jesus is standing in front of you right now.

He is aware of your condition; He knows exactly what you have been struggling through for so long, and He is asking that same searching question of you: "Do you want to get well?"

The choice is yours. After reading this far, you undoubtedly know that your Designer loves you; that He has given you Designer Genes. You know that He has a design for your life, and that He is able to help you complete that plan. You know that if you simply reach out in faith to Him, He is able to perform far greater miracles in and through your life than you could ever imagine. Now that you know, what are you going to do?

How about it? Do you really want to be better?

Jesus says, "I am willing . . . Are you?"

Then don't wait another minute to start living up to your Designer Genes potential. *Get up and walk!*

Inside Out for
"Do You Want to Be Better?"

1. *Break your routine today! Do something different. What are some things you have been wanting to do for a long time but just never have gotten to them? What steps can you take toward doing those things within the next twelve months?*

2. *Recall five painful experiences that have helped shape you into the person you are today. How did your Designer help you through each case?*

3. *What does your will have to do with being well?*

4. *What excuses have you been using to rationalize your ineffectiveness for the Lord?*

5. *Procrastination is a plague with which we are all familiar. Is there something you have been putting off that you know you need to do now? What steps can you take, starting today, to get it done?*

6. *You will be remembered not by how many times you have failed, but by your achievements. Find out how many times Babe Ruth struck out. Compare that to the number of home runs he hit.*

7. *Read the story of "The Prodigal Son" in Luke 15:11–32. What strikes you as the turning point in the story?*

8. *Can you think of any other people who have inhibited your spiritual progress? What can you do today to make up for their influence?*

9. *What alterations do you believe your Designer would like to make on you?*

10. *Remind yourself every day: "God is greater!" (See 1 John 4:4).*

Suggested Reading List

Grant, Dave. *The Ultimate Power.* Old Tappan, New Jersey: Fleming H. Revell Company, 1983.

Mager, Robert F. and Peter Pipe. *You Really Oughta Wanna.* Belmont, California: Pitman Learning, Inc., 1970.

Menninger, Karl. *Whatever Became of Sin?* New York: Hawthorn Books, 1976.

McDowell, Josh. *His Image ... My Image.* San Bernardino, California: Here's Life Publishers, Inc., 1985.

Peters, Thomas and Robert Waterman. *In Search of Excellence.* New York: Harper & Row, Inc. Publishers, 1982.

Schuller, Robert H. *Tough Times Never Last, But Tough People Do!* Nashville, Tennessee: Thomas Nelson Publishers, 1983.

Seamands, David A. *Healing for Damaged Emotions.* Wheaton, Illinois: Victor Books, 1981.

Wagner, Maurice. *The Sensation of Being Somebody.* Grand Rapids: Zondervan Publishing House, 1975.

Waitley, Denis. *Seeds of Greatness.* Old Tappan, New Jersey: Fleming H. Revell Company, 1983.

Ziglar, Zig. *See You at the Top.* Gretna, Louisiana: Pelican Publishing Company, 1974.